Dears

I have so enjoyed getting to know you. We will miss you so much!

Re-zest yourself.
Spiral up.
Move free
@ ♡
Deb

Aug 1, 2018

Dearest Jessica,
I want so much for
you to know that
we will miss you
much.

☺

love,
dad

Moving Free

*A Trail Guide for
Your Ascending Journey*

By Deb Vaughan Ritter

BALBOA
PRESS
A DIVISION OF HAY HOUSE

Copyright © 2017 Inspirations Ink, LLC

All rights reserved. No part of this book may be used or reproduced by any means, graphic, electronic, or mechanical, including photocopying, recording, taping or by any information storage retrieval system without the written permission of the author except in the case of brief quotations embodied in critical articles and reviews.

Balboa Press books may be ordered through booksellers or by contacting:

Balboa Press
A Division of Hay House
1663 Liberty Drive
Bloomington, IN 47403
www.balboapress.com
1 (877) 407-4847

Because of the dynamic nature of the Internet, any web addresses or links contained in this book may have changed since publication and may no longer be valid. The views expressed in this work are solely those of the author and do not necessarily reflect the views of the publisher, and the publisher hereby disclaims any responsibility for them.

The author of this book does not dispense medical advice or prescribe the use of any technique as a form of treatment for physical, emotional, or medical problems without the advice of a physician, either directly or indirectly. The intent of the author is only to offer information of a general nature to help you in your quest for emotional and spiritual well-being. In the event you use any of the information in this book for yourself, which is your constitutional right, the author and the publisher assume no responsibility for your actions.

Any people depicted in stock imagery provided by Thinkstock are models, and such images are being used for illustrative purposes only. Certain stock imagery © Thinkstock.

Print information available on the last page.

ISBN: 978-1-5043-7790-4 (sc)
ISBN: 978-1-5043-7792-8 (hc)
ISBN: 978-1-5043-7791-1 (e)

Library of Congress Control Number: 2017905068

Balboa Press rev. date: 07/06/2017

I am honored to dedicate this book to
my sweet mother, Boydine,
who passed on in the spring of 1997.

I was blessed to be with her during her final weeks
as she floated between her earthly obligations,
visions of her long-departed mother, and her next destination,
with its promise of freedom and light.

And to my precious Pappy, my grandfather,
who always made me feel cherished.
I sense his presence and guidance as
I discover my own true trek.

Contents

Acknowledgments ix
Introduction x

Part I: My Path to Moving Free 1
I Was Born to Move Free—and So Were You 3

Part II: Your Trail Guide for Moving Free 17
Embracing Your Own True Trek 21

> Trail Marker One: Removing the Roadblocks 23
>
> Trail Marker Two: Moving Free in Relationships 34
>
> Trail Marker Three: Your Quest for Your
> Intended Life Purpose 61
>
> Trail Marker Four: When Storm Clouds Gather 76
>
> Trail Marker Five: The Simplest Little
> Meditation Guide Ever! 94
>
> Trail Marker Six: Imagine Moving Free! 101

Part III: Now Can You Imagine Moving Free? 125
The Ride of Your Life 128
Suggested Reading List 131
About the Author 133

Acknowledgments

Mom, I am so grateful to you for sharing your final declaration, *"I must move free!"* I was honored to witness your liberation. Your surprising words transformed the trajectory of my entire life!

I appreciate the love and support of my family during this long creative journey. Craig, you are my rock. You supported me in so many ways and embraced my need for freedom to complete this book. Tyler and Lauren, you believed in me and encouraged me to follow this dream.

Thank you to my talented graphic designers, Shirley Harryman at Stonehouse Studio and Kelly Ludden of Kelly Ludden Design, and to my skilled, collaborative editors: Sunny Dawn Summers, Stacie Tindle, and Julie Tenenbaum (yes, it took three). And thank you to my author coach Diane Gedymin at The Publisher's Desk, who guided me at the beginning of my journey to create a readable whole from my heartfelt but scattered words. Each of your unique contributions to make my first book the best it could be were synergistic and invaluable.

I also want to acknowledge my precious friends, extended family, teachers, healers, and mentors—you know who you are. The laughter, tears, and life experiences we shared helped me learn to move free.

I am especially grateful to my soul-niece Stacie for demonstrating that the principles of *moving free* can be positively life changing, and to my soul sisters—Betty, Kelli, Melodie, and Paula for sharing this journey of awakening with me. Your wisdom, passion, joy, and unconditional love continue to illuminate my path!

Introduction

Can You Imagine Moving Free?

Would you love to liberate yourself from:

- regrets about the past?
- anxiety, depression, or worries about the future?
- feelings of being stuck or hopeless?
- addictions to toxic relationships or substances?
- people who try to control you?
- work and social situations that bind you?
- financial woes?
- difficulty in creating your new reality following a major life shift?

Now is your time to begin moving free toward the life of your dreams by:

- overcoming your obstacles to moving free
- embracing who and what you were meant to be
- developing and renewing joyful, affirming relationships
- loving the work that you do
- manifesting what you desire
- welcoming each day with gratitude and joy
- re-zesting yourself

Your trail guide to moving free awaits. Pick up your backpack and let's get started!

My Journey and Intention

Just before she died, my mother emphatically declared that she had to *move free*. Given that she was anything but a free spirit during her lifetime, this surprising revelation pierced my heart and made me consider whether I was moving free in my own busy life. The indisputable answer was no.

Since her passing, my mother's unintentional legacy has become the impetus for my own remarkable journey of awakening. At long last, I can honestly say I'm moving free – right here, right now – every precious day of my life.

Now it's time for me to hold up the light by sharing this secret gift of self-liberation with you and yours via my personal metamorphosis, my original affirmations and poetry, and my life-coaching tips. My intention is that the magical mysteries of moving free will resonate with you, empower you to recapture your free spirit within, and illuminate your own true trek.

The following poem captures the incredible turning point in my life when it first dawned on me that my mother died with regret and sadness, never having allowed her truest and highest self to emerge. Spending her last few weeks with my mother turned out to be both a blessed obligation and a sacred time of revelation.

I Must Move Free!

She whispered, eyelids fluttering,
a brief awakening from a deep unconsciousness
or perhaps her most conscious moment ever.
A revelation, a flash of clarity,
a simple phrase, not of this world.
I must move free.

It was her final letting go
of fear and the need to fix, to calm the storms
for her own peace had eluded her too long.
What she must do was suddenly clear.
She had glimpsed the God-light coming into view.
I must move free!

Softly she called, *Mommy!*
and warmed to this new gift,
unwrapping it with care.

Meeting her true self face to face
the essence that would endure –
she knew she'd been tethered far too long.

A step, a half-leap
from the pain of her spent body,
her suffering of spirit, her exhaustion.

She embraced her sweet freedom so elusive 'til then.
Her pain dissolved in a flash of light.
In one joyful leap, she was on her way!
No looking back, I must move free, her soul rejoiced.
Her spirit soared as she exclaimed,
I'm moving free!

My Mother's Surprising Legacy

Before my mother passed on, she was anything but a free spirit. She had felt trapped in a long and difficult marriage, and before her death she was ill for many years. So for her, moving free from her pain and suffering was a joyous choice, and passing on was a blessed release from her stressful life. Having spent those final weeks with her, I was able to go past the sadness of losing her, accept what she must do, and even celebrate that she was moving on.

After her death, I felt a sense of relief that her spirit had finally been set free. I recognized her prophetic words—I must move free—were a declaration of self-liberation. I knew they came from a place deep in her soul. Perhaps it was the clearest insight she had ever had. It was certainly the most heartfelt thought she had ever shared with me. Did she speak her epiphany out loud as a confirmation to her self that is was time for her to go? Or was her intention to warn me to commence moving free in my hectic life while I had the chance? I'm not sure.

It seemed to me that she spent her entire life doing exactly what she was expected to do. Typical of many women of her generation, she put others above herself, to a fault. As a result, she didn't claim her personal power or make time to enjoy the simple pleasures of life. I have no doubt that losing her own mother at the age of ten set the stage for her style of homemaking. She occupied herself with creating the illusion of the perfect home and family. She overcompensated for her lack of mothering by providing a nicely decorated house, fashionable clothes, and tasty food for us. In other words, she furnished all the exterior indicators of a happy home. But I seldom felt a strong emotional connection to her. I can't recall her ever being a confidant when I had problems with friends or taking me to lunch or on a walk just to talk.

Of course, I can only speak for myself. Although I don't know the depth of her emotional connection with my brother Tim, it appeared to me that she was much closer to him. I'm sure that his life-changing bout with polio had a profound effect on their personal bond.

I'll never forget the last time her dear and only sister, Jeanne, came to visit her in the hospital. She sat by her bedside for hours, holding her hand and passionately sharing memories of their times together over the years. My mother had assumed a maternal role toward Jeanne following their mother's death, and my aunt treasured those last moments with her loving sister-mom. Even though my mother couldn't respond verbally to her stories, I have no doubt that her spirit heard her sister's recollections and that they warmed her weary heart.

I desperately tried to emulate my aunt's comforting conversation after she returned home—with little success. The sad realization that I could not remember any sweet times of one-on-one sharing with my mom during my childhood spoke volumes.

After racking my brain, I finally came up with a story to share with her. During my grade school days, we raised a litter of Dalmatian pups. I can still feel the joy of playing with those adorable puppies with my mother and the warmth of the sun on our faces as they cavorted and showered sloppy kisses on us. It was a wonderful memory—but that was the only one I could recall.

The exercise of trying to recall pleasant memories was quite an eye-opener for me. It revealed another unsettling insight: Her efforts to be seen as a model mother, wife, and homemaker by others consumed all her time and energy. This was the first of the many aha-moments I experienced in the years following her death.

Naturally, I then questioned whether I was emotionally available to my own children. Some deep soul-searching was called for. Although I was a full-time working mother with limited free time, I knew I was more present with them when we were together than my mother had been with me. My husband Craig and I tried our best to encourage our children to be true to themselves and to pursue their unique talents and destinies.

A plaque I bought when our children were young resonated with me and became my mantra for my parenting style. It read, "There are but two things we must give our children: One is roots, the other wings," and I did my best to provide both for our children. They have both grown into productive, loving adults, pursuing their own talents and finding compatible spouses. The roots and wings we strived to provide must have worked their magic, even though we surely fell short of ideal parenting from time to time. We continue to share heart-warming times with them and their spouses.

My relationship with my mother blossomed once I became a mother myself. She helped me by babysitting when she could and made time for us in her later years. We enjoyed some lovely holidays together and forged many happy memories during that period.

She was a loving grandmother to our children, spending a great deal of time with them in her flower garden and taking them on frequent outings to shop and to feed the ducks at a nearby park. She would cancel her volunteer and social activities when we visited Wichita to take them to the zoo. Our grown children treasure their childhood memories of Nanno to this day.

Perhaps her time with her grandchildren sparked a desire for the deeper emotional bonds she allowed herself later in life with a few close friends. These women provided solace and emotional support that had been lacking in her earlier relationships.

My mother also gave back to the community in some meaningful ways. She used her design, gardening, and floral arranging skills to the benefit of the local ballet company, art museum, and botanical gardens. She used her artistic bent and charisma to contribute to the city she loved. I asked the minister to include my words in her eulogy to describe her considerable volunteer work: "She left the world a more beautiful place than she found it."

My stepsister Sue and I honored her with a garden party following her large formal funeral. About a week prior to her passing, she had asked me if her pink dogwood trees were blooming. It was a delightful surprise that her dogwoods were in full bloom on the day of this celebration of her life. The blossoms were literally floating down on us as her family and friends gathered in her garden to celebrate their special memories of Boydine.

Dogwood Blossoms Floating Down

Dogwood blossoms floating down, floating down,
as she lingered with us there.
Her angel wings must have brushed the trees
as she made her way to *moving free*.

Before the grieving, before the loss,
before the emptiness she left with us,
we hosted a party, in Boydine's style.
Loved ones gathered to celebrate awhile.

We pronounced her "the queen," for a diva she was,
holding court with both style and grace.
She addressed each detail with the utmost care
making sure each guest felt welcomed there.

We shared sweet memories of occasions held
in the garden that was her heart.
Our rainy wedding, reunions, and children at play,
echoed with laughter and tears that day.

Dogwood blossoms floating down, floating down
as she lingered with us there.
Her angel wings must have brushed the trees
as she made her way to *moving free*.

Although I was encouraged as I observed my mother's deepening connection to me, our family, her friends, and the community in her later years, I still strongly sensed that she had never fully embraced her inner free spirit. Grasping the importance of her final revelation—I must move free—I tucked it away in my heart and promptly returned to my own busy life as a wife, mother, and career woman.

All these years later, I've come to understand that those four simple words were her greatest legacy to me. It's been a long and winding road. After many years of solitary reading, meditating, praying, and spiritually searching, the eyes of my heart have opened to the wisdom of her words. It has given me a fresh perspective on the importance of living life to the fullest every day.

It's finally clear to me. I can honor her parting words by moving free, right here and right now, in my own life. This mantra has become the guiding principle for my amazing new journey. I make a choice every day to embrace my path with gratitude. Rather than attempting to dictate outcomes, I look forward to life's intriguing twists and turns. It makes me smile to think of my mother joyfully watching me as I move free in mind, body, and spirit every day.

My Mother's Revelation

Her mystic message—*I must move free!*
called out to me later
amidst my own adversity.

It seemed a natural bend in my life's path
when I realized her heartfelt words
were also meant for me!

It came in a moment—I knew what I had to do.
I would honor her memory, her sweet legacy,
by embracing life fully each new and wondrous day.

So I'm moving free, right here, right now,
treasuring life's synchronicity.
Being true to myself has *set me free!*

PART I
MY PATH TO MOVING FREE

I Was Born to Move Free— and So Were You

When I first began sharing my new life mantra, moving free, in my writing, I believed my journey began with my separation from my husband, my mother's death-bed declaration, and the wake-up call I experienced following my cancer treatment. And indeed, each of those moments bolstered my desire to liberate myself. In retrospect, however, I have come to realize that I was born to move free and to illuminate others' journeys to find their own path toward freedom. Holding up the light for others through my writing is my life's purpose—the reason I am here on earth this time around.

The things we love as a child provide clues for our desired direction as adults. Although I was bound by the rigid familial and societal restrictions inherent in the 1950s, I felt an innate yearning deep within my spirit to liberate myself from those limits. We are all free spirits when we are young children. Certain activities and interactions particularly excite us. Recalling our fondest memories is not only a joyful exercise; it also reveals our natural talents and passions. As you read about some of my fondest memories, allow your own childhood memories to flood back in.

Mud Pies in the Backyard

Our family moved to Great Bend, Kansas, when I was four. I spent many hours making mud pies in the backyard of our new home. I can still feel the gooey warmth of the damp mud in my tiny hands. I molded it into perfect pancakes and left them on the step stones to cook in the blazing sun. I recall playing with the neighbor kids with not a care in the world. I also remember (or perhaps my mother told me) that I insisted upon wearing clean, ironed dresses to go outside to play, but on mud pie days I must have thrown caution to the wind and moved free from my little-girl dress code. Fully immersing myself in these carefree outdoor pleasures was a welcome release from the rigidity of our home. Escaping into nature remains an important way to ground myself even now.

Chartreuse and Purple Outfits

Wearing the brightly colored matching outfits my mother and Aunt Jeanne made for my cousin Kathy and me was another special treat. They featured peasant blouses and tiered, gathered skirts outlined in rickrack. We refused to take them off, ignoring the popsicle stains and sweat, until our mothers insisted it was bath time and snatched them away.

When I was older, I took sewing lessons, which spurred me on to design and fabricate clothes and pillows. Perhaps this was an indication of my independent fashionista tendencies, my earliest appreciation for color, design, and creation. As an adult, I've come to justify my colorful, Bohemian wardrobe as an undeniable artistic expression. My current penchant for creative dressing and design can surely be traced back to those beginning attempts to move free of the style boundaries of the times.

Magical Moments with Pappy

In my early childhood I adored spending time with my paternal grandfather, Pappy. I was sheltered from my maternal grandfather because he was a hoarder and an alcoholic. Since my maternal grandmother died when my mother was young, and my maternal Gammy died when I was three, Pappy was the only constant grandparent in my life. He was the polar opposite of my father, who was a strict disciplinarian. I felt cherished and loved by my Pappy right up until his death.

He lived in a modest home in Wichita with a splendid backyard featuring a garden, a graceful weeping willow tree, and a soothing glider. I was allowed to sleep on the screened-in porch. In the early morning, he would bring me one of his crisp white dress shirts to wear as a robe. We'd head out to the sunny backyard to tend to his black-eyed Susans and other flowers. We would often sit silently on the glider together. After dinner, he took my brother and me on walks, during which we always enjoyed the guilty pleasure of chewing Juicy Fruit gum. Combining this with my middle name, Duér, he created his pet name for me: "Deborah Du'air with gum in her hair." He called my brother, Timothy Michael, "Timothy Mickle, the Great Bend dill pickle," because we both adored the huge kosher ones he bought for us at a local deli. When I recall those idyllic visits, I feel aglow with the light he brought into my small, difficult world. To this day, I find it soothing to garden and take walks with my loved ones.

Bonding Times with Timmy

Timmy was a loving older brother. He made me feel protected and admired. He was stricken with polio at the age of four, which forever changed the course of his life and that of our family. He had to endure multiple surgeries and wear braces during most of his childhood. My mother naturally expended a great deal of energy and time caring for him during his illness. As a result, she might have over-mothered him. They remained closely bonded, right up to the moment she passed on.

Timmy and I were very different in our interests and abilities. He loved to read and learn and was an A student. He spent a lot of time making very detailed drawings of buildings. He enjoyed both competitive sports and intellectual pursuits, including basketball, tennis, science fair competitions, and debate teams. He had some close friends who shared his brilliance and interests.

Despite our differences, we had a pleasant sibling bond and enjoyed horseback riding, visits with Pappy, and church youth group activities together. Following in Tim's scholastic footsteps, however, was no picnic. Many of my teachers were excited when they learned I was Tim Vaughan's little sister. They must have been disappointed when they realized I did not have Tim's passion for scholarly pursuits. I studied just enough to make Bs. My preference for physical freedom and daydreaming took precedence over learning.

As high school came to a close, I rebelled yet again and chose to attend Kansas State University rather than the University of Kansas, where Tim was studying. This came as quite a shock to my father, since I was born in Lawrence while he was a student at KU, and he fully expected me to continue the tradition.

Carefree Escapes

Peggy, my best friend since age eight, was my partner in crime and innocent play throughout my childhood. When my Dad bought horses, she always tagged along on horseback rides and family trips to horse shows. We would laugh so hysterically together that we would end up with our mouths wide open, emitting no sound whatsoever. Although my Dad had a short fuse for most noise I made, even he couldn't resist the laughing fits Peggy and I shared. For me, they provided a welcome break from the countless moments of walking on eggshells in my father's presence.

Peggy and I had a secret hideaway a few blocks from our houses. We would pack a lunch, jump on our bikes, and head to this spot after school or on lazy summer days. It was only a small, shaded vacant lot, but it was a delightful retreat for us. Here we could invent a pretend world and play without restrictions for hours on end.

I often escaped to another sanctuary to get away from the discord in our household, a sheltering weeping willow tree a few houses away. It was the perfect size for climbing, so I settled into its branches for solitude from time to time. My current need for road trips in my Mini Cooper and my love of weeping willow trees hearken back to such pleasant childhood escapes.

Dancing – Sweet Liberation

The dance groups I joined during junior high and high school provided yet another turning point in my early march toward moving free. These dance lessons and parties were provided by Hazel, a brilliant woman who taught ballroom dancing in her basement studio directly across the street from my school. I not only shone as a natural dance partner, I even garnered some ribbons at the monthly dance contests. This prepared me for the homecoming dances, proms, and cheerleading that would become highlights of my high school years.

It followed that all my boyfriends in high school and college had to be good dancers. I was shy and awkward on first dates, but once I stepped onto the dance floor, my light shone brightly. Besides, dancing often led to kissing. My husband Craig took me out to dine and dance on our first date. The kissing wasn't bad, either.

To this day, I love to dance, moving freely in dance clubs with girlfriends or Craig. Sometimes I take our cat Boo for a whirl around our kitchen island, but he finds the dizzying experience to be frightening and quickly escapes my grasp.

Happy Horsey Days

My Dad had always wanted a horse when he was a child, and he purchased several when I was seven. Later he fulfilled his lifelong dream of owning a place on the outskirts of town with a barn and horses grazing just steps from our back door. I loved having the horses so close at hand and did my part with the chores. I spent so much time petting and bonding with one of the colts that she actually followed me into the house one day.

During junior high I took riding lessons from Sandra Bess, a young woman from New Mexico, who worked as a trainer at an Appaloosa ranch owned by the Townsley family. I worked out on the horses three hours a day in rain, shine, or snow in preparation for traveling with Sandra and the Townsleys to show horses. During several summers, we loaded up people and horses and trekked to shows in New Mexico, Missouri, and Iowa. For the first time, I experienced the joys of being part of a large, raucous family. Sandra had a strong influence on me during those early teenage years. She became the big sister I never had, as well as my coach and mentor. She taught me to focus on one thing at a time. Her guidance and acceptance made her a welcome and positive presence in my life. Visiting different states also broadened my world-view and spawned my lifelong love of travel.

On a trip to New Mexico, a jockey at one of the horse shows befriended me. We had much in common, and talking to him was effortless. Although we may have kissed a few times, I had no idea he was actually falling for me. Several weeks after I returned home, he and his sister showed up at the Appaloosa ranch one afternoon just as I was finishing my workout. I was completely shocked and unsettled to realize that he had taken our harmless flirtation seriously. My father had a stern discussion with him, and he and his sister left the next day. For once my Dad really stepped up and rescued me, and I was touched by his concern. It was a rare moment in which I felt unconditional love from him. This incident revealed my small-town naiveté and taught me to be more wary of young men.

For the most part, my travels with the Townsleys were light-hearted and rewarding. The teamwork and mutual admiration of my fellow equestrians gave me a sense of belonging. The comfort of that family feeling warmed my heart. At the same time, my horseback riding escapades enabled me to fulfill my desire for freedom.

Old Santa Fe Rodeo Queen

Although my interest shifted from horses to boys during high school, my Dad was a director of the local rodeo and convinced me to participate in it my senior year. I had not ridden for three years, but I knew this was important to him, and it would likely be the last hurrah in my horseback-riding career. Looking back, some of the best moments in our father-daughter relationship happened during the time we spent together with the horses.

I borrowed a horse, took a short refresher course from my treasured mentor Sandra, and competed in the rodeo queen contest. What a dangerous and dramatic entrance I made that sweltering summer night. I'll never forget the rush of galloping at break-neck speed around the perimeter of the arena, as close to the fence as possible, when I was introduced during the competition. I leaned precariously out over the crowd, smiling and waving in a regal manner. I won the title of Old Santa Fe Rodeo Queen that year. Trying to make my father proud was often futile, but this time I struck gold. I don't think my father was ever more proud of me than the moment I was crowned. What a triumph!

It Wasn't Free and Easy at Home

Most families are dysfunctional in one way or another, and my family of origin was no exception. My father was very critical of my brother and me. His anger often bubbled over, and he sometimes became verbally and emotionally abusive, while my mother acted as the perpetual peacemaker. Although she was a good mother in terms of the trappings, her obsession with impressing others consumed much of her time. And my brother's polio challenges and her social obligations left little time to attend to me, her annoyingly independent daughter.

My parents always provided us with a nice home and financial security, which I don't take for granted. We had much of what we needed to flourish in terms of experiences and opportunities, thanks to my father's successful career. But my parents' relationship was sometimes tumultuous, and they divorced during my freshman year in college.

One of the most important life lessons for moving free is letting go of past woes. I may have carried this to an extreme in some cases by repressing bad memories as a necessary coping mechanism. But as a child who was always on high alert when I was in my father's presence, I began to hone my ability to flip to my other persona—the lively friend and bright student—when I left the house. I chose not to waste my time by dwelling on painful encounters with him.

Thankful for my more freewheeling, post-high-school life and having a naturally resilient nature, I tried to accept that my parents did the best they could, given their own issues. I sought intense counseling much later, which finally allowed me to release anger I still harbored for their shortcomings and to forgive them for the angst I had felt throughout my childhood. I've also come to realize how fortunate I was that the parents of some of my friends took me under their wings and modeled healthy adult relationships as well as the joys of good marriages and parenting skills. What would I have done without them?

Deb Vaughan Ritter

Always Moving Free

Even then, against all odds, I chose to move free.
I squelched my rebellion, but I clung to my will.
I appeared compliant, but I was resolute.

When he locked me inside his prison of intimidation,
I found the dungeon keys and plotted my escape.
I liberated my spirit, time and time again.

He sometimes silenced my voice,
but he never crushed my yearning.
He suppressed my spirit, but he never broke it.

I stitched my craving for freedom
safely inside my pocket of hope.
Somehow those frayed seams held tight.

My fragile child-self always conspired to escape.
I somehow managed to break free from my cell.
I plotted diversions. I stole myself away.

Whether galloping into the dust on my horse,
climbing into the womb of my willow tree,
or dancing with abandon—I found a way.

It's crystal clear to me at last.
Even then I chose to *move free*.
I always did. I always will.

Wild and Crazy College Days

I spent the last few years of high school anticipating and planning my escape from Great Bend and my family. Rather than being fearful of what the future held, I couldn't wait to spread my wings. Long before I discovered its true meaning, I had an undeniable urge to move free.

During my early days at Kansas State University in Manhattan, Kansas, dubbed "The Little Apple," it took some time to come into my own, given the many years I consciously self-edited my thoughts before I uttered anything to my father. Whereas I had been one of the cool kids in high school, safe within my clique, college was a bigger, more intimidating world. My friend Melodie, who had talked me into going to KSU and rooming with her, gave me comfort and direction. With her support, I could finally drop my guard and explore this exciting new world.

I made some interesting friends. College was all about dates with lots of adorable boys and playing bridge in the student union between classes. What a guilty pleasure that was for me. Pledging a sorority gave me a closer circle of security and many set-ups for blind dates. Looking back, on some level, I think I was particularly drawn to some of my sisters because they were already moving free. Those friendships enriched my college experience by allowing me to rediscover my natural playfulness.

Despite all these temptations, I attended all my classes and prioritized my study time. Melodie insisted upon regular study hours during the week, and I willingly followed her lead. As a result, I made a 3.8 GPA that first semester, a vast improvement over the B average of my high school days. It was a surprising accomplishment, and my sorority appreciated this contribution to our house GPA as well.

When I was deciding on a major, I reflected on my fascination with the mind and personality of others. Why was my Aunt Marcia so jovial and sweet? She had been raised in the same household as my brooding father. Why couldn't all men be as pleasant and accepting as my Pappy? Why did I always feel the need to play the role of therapist for my friends during high school and college? Why did I spend so much time writing poetry about my friends and boyfriends?

Studying psychology and philosophy and getting in touch with my inner hippie during my college years couldn't have been more liberating. I read existentialist books voraciously. Nothing pleased me more than long discussions about these exciting new concepts, but I always managed to fit dancing, dating, and bridge into my schedule. What good was my newly discovered sense of freedom if I couldn't express it in all aspects of my outrageously exciting life?

On the flip side, it was crystal clear that my independence was dependent upon doing what was expected of me—getting a degree in four years and securing a job. I was ever so motivated to do so, because I couldn't wait to begin my life as a grownup. I graduated with honors with a Bachelor of Arts in Psychology and landed a lucrative job in Kansas City. Moving into an apartment with my flight attendant roommate and starting a career were joyful leaps toward moving free.

It's Your Turn to Reflect

I encourage you to recapture both the joy and pain of your youth as you embark upon your journey toward moving free. Take a few moments and do your own digging for memories and influences.

You may wish to journal or sketch your discoveries or create a scrapbook or collage of photos from your childhood. Whatever the method, these questions might help you rediscover your early interests and hobbies and the types of people who molded you into the adult you are:

- *Who had a particularly life-changing effect on you, either positive or negative?*
- *Were there particular teachers, coaches, relatives, or mentors who helped you stretch and grow?*
- *In what concrete ways has their influence manifested in your current life?*
- *How did the size (small town vs. city) and location of your hometown affect you?*
- *Were you eager to leave your home (physically and emotionally) or were you content to stay?*
- *What pivotal moments changed your life in a major way?*
- *How did specific circumstances of your youth shape you as an adult?*
- *What interests and activities resonated with you? What talents and passions emerged during your childhood?*
- *Have you incorporated those talents and passions into your current life?*

Your exciting trek toward moving free awaits. The trailhead is just ahead. Let's hit the road.

PART II

YOUR TRAIL GUIDE FOR MOVING FREE

Caution: You Are Entering a Judgment-Free Zone

Self-judgment often bubbles up when you begin a journey of awareness and change. The intention in this book, however, is to illuminate your path and lift you up, not to make you feel inadequate or judged. Gently remind yourself that you are on a pathway to loving and accepting precisely where you are at this moment on your sacred journey.

The practical principles for moving free in your mind, body, and spirit are accessible to all, regardless of your age or stage in life. This book isn't intended to change your current belief system. This information can be framed within the context of any religious or spiritual orientation.

Deb Vaughan Ritter

Please read this poem from the bottom to top, as if you were climbing a mountain path.

My Ascending Journey

Ah!
bliss.
my sweet
the way *to my true trek,*
Trusting my intuition —

pointing to my dream-life.
an important trail marker
Envisioning a desired outcome —

on the journey toward *moving free.*
Accepting what is — a crucial step

paved with suffering and pain.
Resisting what is — a rough road

a direct path to resistance and frustration.
Attempting to control people and situations —

Embracing Your Own True Trek

When my husband and I were dating, we drove to Breckenridge, Colorado, with his brother Steve and sister-in-law Jeanne for a summer vacation. Before we met, Craig had lived in Denver and had spent a great deal of time skiing and hiking in the Rockies, so he was excited about hiking with me from Copper Mountain to Breckenridge. I knew the views and the experience would be spectacular. Although I was unsure if I was physically up for the challenging twelve-mile hike, I sensed it would be a turning point in our blossoming love affair.

The front face of the mountain, four miles in length, revealed a gorgeous and steep trail through the forest enhanced by babbling brooks and lovely wildflowers. This initial portion of the hike was particularly difficult for me because of its steep vertical climb, but the beauty and romantic adventure of it all urged me on. I was a real trooper during the beginning of our ascent, partly because I knew the front face was only one-third of the hike, and the gentler descent on the ski slopes of Breckenridge promised to be a piece of cake once we reached the top.

About halfway up the front face, the trees receded, and an easier trail unfolded before us. Although it wasn't as visually appealing as the first section, the hiking became easier because of the more gradual incline. Or so I thought. Soon my muscles ached, the sun blazed, and the fleeting glimpse of what I believed to be the summit disappeared to reveal yet another peak. For the next long hour, like mirages in the desert, one summit after another came into sight and vanished. My exhaustion finally got the better of me.

More than once Craig had paused when he realized I wasn't following closely behind him. He would turn around to check on me, only to find me lying on the ground, defeated in the belief that I couldn't take one more step. Each time he patiently let me relax, encouraging me with promises that the actual peak was just ahead and a picnic lunch and a nice long rest awaited me at the top of the mountain. He couldn't take the necessary steps for me. He couldn't throw me over his shoulder and carry me. He knew it. I knew it. I alone had to muster the courage, determination, and energy to keep on trekking.

Like climbing a steep mountain trail, just when we think we have our life plan figured out, yet another challenge or possibility suddenly appears. Like a bend in the path of a challenging hike, we're sometimes momentarily thrown off course or we want to stop and not take another step. That's why it's so important to choose like-minded individuals with whom to share our walk through life. We will sometimes lead the way and at other times step back and allow others to do so. We will encourage each other, but ultimately we alone must choose our own direction, keep going when we desperately want to turn back, and finally, with patience and determination, discover our own true north.

Despite most people's tendency to focus on the destination, it's not just about arriving at the summit. Embracing our upwardly spiraling path and celebrating our ever-expanding vistas is what really matters. While it is helpful to reset your intention for a desired outcome from time to time, if we concentrate too much on the end goal, we may miss the wonderful sights and sounds of the hike itself.

Trail Marker One: Removing the Roadblocks

Since we are starting at the trailhead of our hike toward moving free, we must begin at the base of our own mountain. Before we can adopt new, more positive perspectives, we must first let go of persistent patterns and habits that block our route to personal liberation. The first step is to stop trying to control people and situations; until we do, we will remain immobilized at the beginning of our journey.

> The moment I choose to relinquish control
> is the very moment in which my dreams begin to unfold.

No matter how strong your urge to control people and situations, you must choose the more liberating path for your mental and spiritual health and for the sake of those you love. Relinquishing control of outcomes is a daunting task when you first attempt it, but doing so is well worth the effort. The sooner you realize it is beyond your ability to make people and situations do your bidding, the sooner you will embark upon the exciting journey of recapturing your free spirit within. You'll begin to feel as if the weight of the world has been lifted from your shoulders; now you're carrying responsibility only for your own actions. With persistence and with a lighter load to carry, you can and will move upward and onward in the direction of your freedom.

The crisis that made me realize I must give up trying to control everything around me was my cancer diagnosis. Although I was shocked and frightened, I had no choice but to accept my diagnosis and realize I was no longer fully in control of my health. Although I could make decisions about my treatment, of course, the bottom line was that I still had to trust my doctors. Instead of constantly second-guessing every decision, I focused on what I could control—maintaining a positive outlook while I charged forward through the recommended treatments and surgeries that followed.

Such wakeup calls knock us down and give us pause. Once I recovered from my cancer treatment and surgeries, I no longer felt compelled to control every aspect in my life. I gradually learned to loosen my grip on many personal and professional situations. The silver lining of my cancer was realizing the world would go on without my constant vigilance; others would and could pick up the slack for me when necessary. It was a great relief and a giant step forward in my long path to personal liberation. Moreover, my family and friends felt freer to explore their own paths without my direction.

As you gradually become reacquainted with your more carefree self, you will begin to take steps toward a more joyful life path. You will begin to recognize the synchronicity that naturally arises in your life. You will realize that a chance meeting with someone who can assist you with your goals or spark a solution to a persistent problem is not accidental. You will accept that an unexpected fork in the road could lead you far beyond the tiny back roads to a super highway of success and happiness. Aren't more positive outcomes worth the effort of relinquishing the habit of trying to control people and situations?

> Letting go of the past by realizing it holds no power over me *frees my spirit* to embrace the joy that is,
> right here, right now.

Quelling the urge to control people and situations indicates real progress on your journey, but there may be other barriers that could block the trail ahead. The next step is releasing regrets about the past by letting go of any lingering pain, anger, or doubts. Continuing to blame yourself or others for past mistakes prevents you from creating the life you desire.

I lost a job I both loved and needed at a top commercial textiles manufacturer; the stated reason was that I had left a sales meeting early. I had made plans to meet a friend in the lobby of the hotel at five o'clock (when our sales meeting was scheduled to end). The meeting ran over, so I left my things in the conference room and dashed out to tell her I was running late. Unfortunately, the meeting wrapped up just after I left, and the Vice President of Sales rounded the corner in time to see me talking to her, giving him the impression that I had left early with no intention of returning. Talk about bad timing!

Although I later learned there were other underlying financial considerations at play, he not only fired me that very evening, he also announced my dismissal to the rest of the sales team the next morning to demonstrate the consequences of failing to take such meetings seriously. During the following weeks, I was haunted by feelings of insecurity and self-judgment. As I worked through and released the pain and humiliation, I was able to land another job as an independent representative. The flexibility of this situation better suited my family's circumstances: I was able to work out of my home office, which meant shorter days, less stress, and more availability for our teenage children.

In retrospect, the outcome was better than I could have engineered. So was my momentary lapse in judgment an unfortunate accident or an example of one door closing in order to provide an opening for a better situation?

The key to removing the debris called regret is to realize that we all make mistakes and do the best we can given the situation, our capabilities, and our limitations. We must absolve ourselves and others in order to move forward. Finally leaving a person or situation that no longer serves you may require overcoming your fear or forgiving someone who has hurt you.

This simple exercise might help when you are having trouble letting go of regret or other unproductive emotions. Make a fist and envision yourself holding that troubling situation tightly inside it. Now open your hand and imagine its contents floating away. It's a useful visual reminder that we have the capacity to release what does not serve us.

What have you got to lose? Imagine moving free, and give it a shot. The free spirit inside you wants to dance. Once you realize the past has no power over you today unless you allow it to, you have access to joy right here, right now.

Just One Step

> It's just one step along my path—
> the footprint will not last.
> Just one small step in my long trek,
> neither my future nor my past.
> I choose to find the meaning
> of the pain I feel today.
> It reveals a bright new secret
> that will always light my way.

Of course, retaining bits of hard-earned wisdom and recollecting pleasant memories is encouraged. Remember—every choice you ever made is just one small step in your long life's journey. And everything that happened to you contributed to who you are today.

> I shall resist the urge to worry,
> realizing it is a destructive force in my life.

We've now moved beyond controlling others and being stuck in the past. Next it's time to clear the roadblock of worrying about the future. If we are overcome by fear of possible negative scenarios in our future, we become immobilized.

Worrying about things we can't control is an incredible waste of our time and energy. Fortunately, there are many ways to release worrisome thoughts: by exercising, breathing deeply, relaxing in nature, reflecting, or meditating. Such activities work because they gently bring our attention back to the present and clear our minds. Doing so allows new, more positive directions to emerge in our consciousness. The point is clear: We can only move free in each present moment. Until we live in the present, we cannot live fully, productively, or joyfully.

Try to catch yourself when you fret about something that hasn't happened yet. Remind yourself that doing so will only bring you down. I've come to believe that nothing is an accident, and that we actually manifest those things—positive or negative—upon which we place our attention. For example, if you spend at least five minutes a day sitting quietly and envisioning yourself doing something that you wish for—sometimes called positive manifesting—you might be delighted to discover that the funds or opportunities to do that activity serendipitously appear in your life. This concept may seem outrageous, but I have experienced it first-hand.

The best illustration of my success with positive manifesting is responding to my urge to write this book. I began hearing a non-verbal voice whispering affirmations and poetry in my ear as I awakened each morning. I immediately captured them on my laptop. Soon I began writing the book in earnest. Next I began identifying myself as a writer. As a result of my desire and this declaration, the most marvelous people and opportunities began showing up—making it possible to fulfill my desire and destiny to be a writer. You hold the proof of my manifestation in your hands.

Consider this: If the power of positive manifesting is real, then the opposite practice would be as well. You may actually be inviting adversity into your life through needless worrying. Be mindful of the adage, "Be careful what you wish for; it might just happen." It's an ancient and simple truth that bears consideration. Often, what you think about will appear, whether it is something wonderful or something dreadful. Why not envision what you desire rather than what you dread?

Sometimes worriers want you to worry with them. Even if you want to ease a friend's pointless worrying, it's impossible to do so, and it's often a slippery slope that can cause you to fall off your path. All you can do is encourage them to let go of worrying about situations they can't control or simply set a good example for them. Ultimately, they must learn to break this limiting habit themselves.

By the time I began writing this book, I had mostly corralled the urge to worry. Had I listened to my own self-doubts or the discouraging comments of others, I would have relinquished my dreams. I chose to believe in my positive inner urgings and myself. I was determined to let this creative venture unfold, regardless of the very real internal fears or external naysayers I encountered.

> Accepting what is, right here, right now,
> is the perfect starting point
> for making my way to *moving free*.

In order to follow a trail guide, we must first identify our current location. If we can't locate our starting point, the map is useless. Similarly, we cannot move free unless we are honest with ourselves about where we stand today. If we don't recognize what is and what isn't working in our lives, how can we possibly move in the direction of our desired relationships, work, and life?

Accepting your circumstances, right here and right now, requires honest self-evaluation. We must face the fact that certain aspects of our life are not entirely satisfying at the moment. What activities and people bring us joy? What or who frustrates us? Being grateful for loving friends and family members who enrich our lives is a good place to start. Once we've dealt with our own weaknesses, we will have more empathy for what others may be going through.

Resistance is the opposite of acceptance. If we are rigidly resisting growth and change, we will never move beyond the beginning of our trail. We will continue to repeat the same frustrating scenarios in our life over and over again until we are able to accept what is true today.

If we are still holding onto control issues that complicate our life and those of our friends and family, we must come to grips with that. If we have an addiction that is standing in the way of our happiness, we must admit that to ourselves and seek help to overcome it. If we keep getting fired or rejected, we must recognize our own repetitive actions that are contributing to that negative outcome. In other words, we must quit blaming others for what is wrong in our life and start being accountable for our own decisions and actions.

As adults, we have the right to live however we wish to live within the norms of society. But we must accept the consequences of our choices. If we continue to deceive ourselves about what is causing our current difficulties, forward motion is hindered. If we catch ourselves thinking or saying, "I will be happy when…," then we aren't accepting our current reality. Or if we say, "If only this hadn't happened…," it is a good indicator that we are living in the past. We must start where we are right now without any excuses before we can navigate toward our desired destination. Once we have cleared such roadblocks, we will be equipped to face the future with honesty. A renewed sense of direction will surface.

In the past, when I became ill, I tried to push through and keep my appointments. Now when I am sick, I choose to face the fact that I feel bad. I cancel my plans and then relax and rest without guilt. I create as cozy a place as possible in which to read, watch television, or nap. I eat and sleep when I feel the need. By letting go of my resistance to my circumstances and accepting them as they are, I can use my energy to heal.

The Weeping Willow

I pause to view a willow tree
its boughs inviting me to rest.
It had survived a man-made plan,
standing strong amidst a builder's scheme.

Drawn to this majestic tree
I lean into its sturdy trunk.
Lingering within its cool canopy
I cherish its sweet solitude.

With its branches gently moving free,
it's wrong to call this willow weeping.
Its delicate boughs wave in the breeze
sharing their free-flowing ease with me.

Are You Bending Like the Willow?

Willow branches aren't heavy and rigid enough to grow parallel to the horizon like most tree branches do. Rather, they are pliable and hang loosely, pulled earthward by the natural force of gravity.

Have you dared to relinquish the unchangeable past and the unknowable future, trusting that your life will unfold as intended? Are you going with the flow of a gentle breeze of change, or are you rigidly holding on to old patterns? Try stepping out in trust and bending like the willow. If you are able to do so, you are beginning to move free.

When we are able to accept what is so at this moment, we are allowing God/Spirit/the Universe to manifest the ideal outcome—one that we might not have imagined from our limited human perspective. Our resistance to a situation also creates resistance in others, while flexibility encourages others to join us on our path. If you step out with courage, you might be pleasantly surprised at the outcomes that appear in your life. Dabbling with the possibilities of bending like the willow is a grand experiment indeed!

Notice how much lighter your backpack feels now that you've offloaded some of your cumbersome baggage of fear and excuses. You have conquered the vertical climb through the heavily forested path. The gentler incline is just ahead. After a brief rest, it's time to keep on trekking.

03 03 03

The following guided questions may help you move free along your path. Quickly journal the first thoughts that come to mind. Recording them is a starting point to setting yourself free.

- *What roadblocks, self-doubts, or excuses are holding you back from moving forward? What painful memories do you cling to in order to justify remaining stuck in your life?*
- *Are you still attempting to control or change certain people in your life—expecting them to fulfill your expectations? List these people and acknowledge in what way you are being controlling in those relationships.*
- *Are you living in the present moment by accepting what is right here, right now?*

- *List some specific resolutions for changes you need to make in order to accept your life as it is now and move in the direction of personal freedom for yourself and for those you care for.*
- *Have you ever relinquished a situation beyond your control and been pleasantly surprised by the outcome? If so, record that pleasant memory.*
- *In what areas do you feel you hang loosely like the branches of a willow tree? Take a moment to celebrate these small victories in your life.*

Trail Marker Two: Moving Free in Relationships

Another important aspect of manifesting a more joyful journey is learning to move free in both personal and professional relationships. This task entails seeking out like-minded friends and co-workers, celebrating and nurturing healthy connections, and limiting or releasing those that don't support our desired growth and freedom. On the flip side, we must be honest enough to recognize our own shortcomings and admit them to others. The bottom line is that we must insist on moving free in all of our relationships, and we must return the favor by allowing others to move free in their own way.

Family of Origin

The influence of our family of origin cannot be overstated. If we were raised in a nurturing environment, our path to happiness as an adult will likely be smoother. If our family of origin wasn't a very loving one, our climb to maturity may be more challenging. There is no such thing as the perfect family. Each family has its share of healthy and dysfunctional aspects. Birth order and gender and other dynamics also affect how we perceive our relationship to others.

I described my childhood earlier. Although I didn't feel emotionally comfortable at home, I compensated for this perceived void by finding other relationships and activities. Children are naturally resilient and learn how to meld into their particular environment. As an adult, I had to consciously forgive my parents in order to release the painful feelings that haunted me during my early adulthood.

If our parents disappointed us or even harmed us in some way, we have two choices: repeat the same patterns, or break the cycle. In other words, we can move free from the undesirable aspects of parenting that we found hurtful. Whether we have acquired the habits of anger, violence, guilt, or shame, releasing such damaging behavior is essential to our wellbeing. If we have children of our own, we can choose to parent in a more loving and affirming way. If we didn't have a model of good parental behavior, we must find direction by observing others, seeking advice, or simply following our gut in order to become fully functional adults who can maintain healthy relationships.

Comforting Connections with Extended Family

The love and nurturing given by our extended families is also crucial to our sense of belonging in our later lives. They say it takes a village to raise a child. The positive influence of loving aunts, uncles, cousins, and grandparents can't be over-emphasized.

I was fortunate to have such people in my life. Since my mother and her sister Jeanne were very close, we often visited back and forth with my cousins on her side of the family. They lived in Salina, Kansas (a quick two-hour drive away). When they came to Great Bend, my brother and I played with our cousins Keith and Kathy and Kim in our unfinished basement. One of our favorite activities was producing skits and plays. The preparations and rehearsals provided endless hours of fun, and the performances held our parents captive for a bit. Tim was the creator and director, and I was in charge of costuming. One particularly fond memory of our summer adventures at the cousins' house was raising tadpoles in a big tub in their backyard. We scurried out one morning to discover tiny frogs jumping around. That was a pretty magical day.

Trekking to our cousins' home on my Dad's side of the family was a much bigger deal, since they lived in Indiana. My cousin Ann was several years older than me, so of course, I idolized her. My cousin Dave was much older. I perceived him as a giant and had a kissing-cousins crush on him for years. They had horses right on their stately property, which featured a long, tree-lined lane with pastures on either side. I first fell in love with horses on these visits. My Aunt Marcia and Uncle Roy Lee were jolly and sweet, much different than my parents. Christmases spent in their idyllic home were carefree and exciting. These capers with my cousins and interactions with my aunts and uncles were joyous interludes that provided a comforting break from the tension at home.

My Pappy also filled in the gaps of unconditional love early in my childhood. Since I didn't have a grandmother after the age of three, my great aunt Dorothy and great uncle Marty also stepped up to provide warmth and stability for my brother and me.

One of the perks of my early relationship with Craig was that his extended family embraced me wholeheartedly. They made me feel a part of their fun-loving and close family. His brother Steve, sister-in-law Jeanne, and their children were excited that Craig had found "the one." We had their blessing, and I melded into their family quickly. Our extended families modeled a happy home, which was particularly important to Craig and me during the early years of our marriage and parenting. Years of joyful holidays and casual times of hanging out followed. We both learned much from them about parenting and making family gatherings light-hearted. When they moved to California and we moved to Kansas City, maintaining the connection became more complicated.

Steve died of complications of diabetes when he was forty-four. This was a huge loss for all of us, especially Craig, who lost his big brother and best friend. Our connection to his family has remained strong. Jeanne traveled to be with me for my first chemo treatment. When we got home from the treatment, she turned on some music and we danced that chemo into my body. I may have felt rough later on, but we chose to welcome this treatment with laughter and dancing—celebrating that it was a life-saving step for me.

Creating My Own Family

I must admit that during my childhood I was sometimes jealous of my friends' families of origin because my own was so harsh. There wasn't much laughter in our home, so I honed my skills in creating my other family. I loved hanging out at my friends' homes where I felt more at ease. My friends provided a safe haven of emotional support and laughter. Their parents accepted me with warmth and encouraged me throughout my early years.

I remember my friend Judy's mom consoling me after a high school boyfriend had broken my heart. She took me out to their back porch to enjoy the warm breeze while we shared a private talk. I think I might have drowned my sorrows with a beer or two earlier in the evening. Her message was simple: "Debbie, there are more fish in the sea." It is a fond memory of the emotional support she gave me.

When our children were teenagers, I returned the favor by welcoming their friends into our home. Some of them seemed to need the additional nurturing that Craig and I offered. To this day, some of their friends still thank us for being such loving "other parents" to them.

It is important for people who are missing the comfort of strong family connections to be open to the possibility of creating their family, as I did. I feel surrounded by love and support from both my blood relatives and my dearest friends.

Fantastic Friendships – Old and New

To paraphrase a saying that occasionally circulates on the Internet: "Friends come into our lives for a reason, a season, or a lifetime." I think there is much truth in this axiom. Friendships ebb and flow as the years pass. Healthy, close friendships exist between like-minded individuals. We sometimes become incompatible because our spiritual beliefs, politics, lifestyle choices, interests, or life paths take different directions. Our conversations no longer resonate as joyfully and comfortably as they once did. This is neither good nor bad, but simply a natural occurrence. Truth be told, continuing to spend a great deal of time with a person because we feel obligated to do so, doesn't serve them or us. A misguided sense of loyalty should never deter us from moving free from a relationship that no longer resonates with both parties.

The Ebb and Flow of Friendships

As you evolve on your path toward moving free
Friendships will come and friendships will go.
It's natural for them to ebb and flow.

Relationships both old and new
will shift a bit—either wither or grow.
Some might naturally fade away.

Evolving relationships are part of your growth.
Some friendships are no longer meant to be
because they deter you from moving free.

Choose to celebrate the friendships
that light up your day
and be content to allow others to drift away.

Some friendships remain important to both people throughout their lifetimes. No matter how long it has been since they saw each other, they quickly and naturally reconnect, as if no time has passed. I have friends with whom I still share this type of friendship. My group of high school girlfriends and I have been enjoying weekend reunions together every fall for more than twenty years. Even though our current lifestyles and politics may not be quite as in sync as they once were, there is an acceptance of each other as we are now. Trust is born out of our long history together. We know each other's deepest and darkest secrets, after all. We can freely laugh and cry together as we support each other through life's ups and downs.

The bond that lingers with those who knew you way back when is reassuring. Such connections may remain strong even though they have been dormant for some time. I have recently rekindled my friendship with Peggy, who was my best friend from age eight through high school. It has been comforting to reconnect. Although our life paths diverged, our friendship still abounds with ease and laughter. Even after thirty years, we are effortlessly transported back into fits of giggling and truth sharing. What an unexpected joy this has been.

Other friendships are based on proximity or common activities. Neighbors might become close friends or remain simply acquaintances. My husband and I met and befriended a number of neighbors as well as parents of our children's friends during the early years in Kansas City. How would we have survived parenthood without the giving and accepting of support from other parents? We still see some of them socially and attend their family milestones. Sharing the joy and responsibility of raising children forged strong bonds that remain intact.

Sometimes we experience an instant connection with a new person we happen to meet along our life journey. These easy friendships are a gift. Such friends are meant to support each other in their similar paths, for a particular reason or at least for a period of time. Or if you believe in reincarnation, as I do, they might seem familiar upon your first meeting because they were an important friend or relative in an earlier lifetime. I believe that such immediate and effortless friendships are an important part of our natural synchronicity (more on that in Trail Marker Six). These unexpected relationships can be positively life changing to achieve our life's purpose.

I experienced this type of meant-to-be friendship a few weeks after we moved to Kansas City. Our doorbell rang one morning, and I opened my door to discover an adorable young woman towing her two small sons in a Red Flyer wagon. She introduced herself as Paula and said she was searching out young families with children in the neighborhood. We immediately hit it off and ended up sharing the joys and trials of raising our children for the next fifteen years. Our kids played together, and she provided nurturing after-school childcare for our kids when I returned to work full-time. Paula remains one of my best friends and soul sisters to this day.

Paula's true trek led her to leave a long-term marriage and create an ultra-simple and secluded life in which she was free to pursue her art in her own time, in her own way. Her home in Topanga Canyon, California, consisted of a decrepit old trailer, a tent bedroom on a wooden platform, and the great out-of-doors. Several years ago I enjoyed a peaceful retreat in her "Lucky Bamboo" space. In the middle of the night, rainfall on the roof of my tent awakened me. I called out to Paula (who was sleeping outside on the platform behind the tent) to come inside with me. Snuggled under her blankets, she continued to sleep as the raindrops fell on her face. I shouted louder, but her slumber remained undisturbed.

I gave up on saving her, for she apparently didn't need to be saved. I grabbed my pillow and scurried into the comfort of the trailer. I awoke early the next morning, thinking, "Paula doesn't have the sense to come in out of the rain." When I shared this with her, she laughed with glee, because her mother had told her the same thing many times during her adventurous youth. Paula assured me that because an owl had flown over her as she fell asleep, she felt protected through the night and rested peacefully.

Can you imagine sleeping soundly despite the rain because an owl flew over you? I'm not so brave as all that, but Paula is. She chooses to live without fear. She must have been an Indian maiden in another life, to trust so deeply in Mother Earth's protection. Few could walk in such courage. Her example constantly gives me pause and urges me forward to boldly try things I've always said I couldn't do. Our meeting was no accident, and our bond runs deep and continues to enrich both our lives.

Another kindred spirit relationship unexpectedly surfaced while I was working as a rep for the commercial textile firm. Kelli and I immediately established an effortless connection and remained in touch after my sudden departure from that job. She spent the years after we worked together trekking toward her destiny of becoming a chiropractor, yoga teacher, and nutritional counselor. She enthusiastically stepped up to be my health and spiritual mentor during my cancer battle and after a car wreck. She came alongside me by healing my body with chiropractic adjustments and nutritional suggestions and healing my mind with words of encouragement.

Kelli's biggest contribution to my evolution came when she invited me to rent a small office in the wellness center she had founded.

It provided a nurturing and joyful space in which I could pursue my writing career. Little did I know what a dramatic and powerful period of growth I would experience within the cocoon of the magical atmosphere she had created. The thought-provoking seminars, workshops, and kirtans (ancient participatory music experiences) at her studio fed my growth and that of countless others. She quietly and humorously encouraged me, providing the rich soil and nutrients to gently help me blossom into the woman I was intended to be. Our continuing friendship is a treasure.

Through Kelli I met yet another soul sister. I was training for my first two-day breast cancer walk when I met Betty, an energy and bodywork healer whose practice room was on the second floor of the yoga studio. I was delighted to learn she lived only a half-mile from me. Our bond was forged during early morning walks. She was patient in going at my slower pace, and we gradually became easy friends as we shared our lives during those walks. Her special style of bodywork and her joyous spiritual growth continue to be blessings in my life. We can count on a smile and a hug and spur-of-the-moment outings in our freewheeling friendship.

Both my long-time friends and newer ones are special to me. The rich tapestry of my life wouldn't be complete without the golden threads of connection each of my friends have contributed. I am especially appreciative of my soul sisters, because we continue to walk our similar journeys as awakened and joyful women. It took years for me to finally discover my tribe, and I whisper a prayer of gratitude for them every day.

Special Spouses and Loving Life Partners

Strong marriages and partnerships based on love and mutual respect are rare gems that provide a sanctuary of comfort in our lives. Such unions include a deep level of commitment and a mutual desire to be true life partners. Although my parents divorced shortly after my high school graduation, some of my relatives and parents of my childhood friends illuminated such lifelong love stories for me.

My friend Peggy recently lost her father, George. She told me her mother, who suffered from Alzheimer's, spent his last afternoon holding hands with him. She grew weary and was wheeled back to her room in the same nursing home just hours before his peaceful passing. Even though her mother couldn't remember what she had done earlier in the day, nothing—not even her advanced dementia and his health problems—could destroy their pure love for each other. What a glowing example of lifelong devotion.

During my early years of marriage and motherhood, I met an older, wiser woman who told me, "If you are married for a long time, you will experience some good, some bad, and even some ugly years with your spouse." And certainly, Craig and I have traversed all those phases in our marriage. We are still together, in part because some of our worst years provided the most urgent vehicle for rapid growth and reconnection through counseling and difficult truth sharing. Although our relationship has ebbed and flowed through the years, we finally arrived at a comfortable plateau of mutual respect, acceptance, and love.

In my opinion, the foundations of successful marriages and partnerships include:

- lifestyle compatibility
- mutual empathy and acceptance
- a desire to partner and support each other through life's ups and downs
- similar spiritual and financial values

- respect for each other's life and career choices
- shared interests enjoyed together
- sexual attraction and deep love

Considering how many important criteria are essential to creating a viable partnership in which both parties "feel the magic," what are the chances of finding "the one"? Slim, indeed.

Perhaps that is what has spawned the popularity of matchmaking services and dating apps. I can see value in those that help you evaluate your compatibility prior to meeting. Even though you may have to kiss a lot of frogs (or frogettes), at least you have a qualified list. Online dating can be fun and fruitful—some relationships have resulted from connecting in this way—but it can also end in heartbreak. In those cases, you need not take it personally or try to figure out what you did wrong. Leave your ego out of it and realize that you simply weren't a good match.

You can't decide to find a life partner and expect it to happen in your timeframe. Loving yourself and doing the things you enjoy will increase your chances of meeting those who share your interests.

When a new couple meets, they might rush into a relationship based primarily on physical attraction. However, it is important that other crucial aspects of a healthy relationship are given time to materialize. It is wise to postpone the sexual connection until after the individuals have learned to relate to each other on a deeper level—particularly if their goal is to be in a monogamous marital relationship.

My parents and many couples who met during the World War II era entered into marriages based on physical attraction and a sense of urgency before building the other components of their relationships. My parents turned out to be incompatible, and their tumultuous marriage ended in divorce after twenty years. My mother told me they continued to be sexually attracted to each other throughout their union. Apparently, that one facet wasn't enough to keep them together.

My friend Melodie married the love of her life following a first marriage to an emotionally abusive man. She and her second husband had worked together for some time before they became involved. Their relationship is a shining example of a well-rounded and strong connection that has endured.

Craig and I met by chance at a potluck dinner. We have shared many joyful years together and weathered some storms, as well. After the initial shock of sudden parenthood subsided, we parented well together. The empty nest has allowed us an opening to new adventures and travel that we both enjoy. We have created a more relaxed and comfortable connection. We have finally become grandparents, and this is perhaps our most joyful collaboration ever! But that's a whole other book in the making.

Thank You, Craig

Thank you, thank you, Craig
for accepting my need to move free
and for embracing that craving, too.
Thanks for making me feel safe
and protecting me with love,
but not squelching my spirit.

Thank you for embracing my need to create—
for gently pointing out the facts
when I prefer focusing on the fun.

Thanks for the adventures—
the ones we've shared together
and those we've allowed each other.

Thank you for growing into fatherhood,
taking over when I needed it most,
and being my rock during crisis.

Thanks for moments of hard truth sharing
when we didn't get each other
and for sometimes letting it go.

Thank you for retreating into your cave
until you felt safe to quietly engage with me.
And for coming out to share when our anger waned.

Thanks for teaching me to laugh at myself,
for often laughing with me,
and for finding my quirks endearing.

Thank you for sometimes being
the wind beneath my wings
while still spreading your own.

Thank you, thank you, Craig
for all you are and do.
It's no wonder I'm still in love with you!

Collaborating Co-workers

Our relationships with co-workers, bosses, and employees are important to our productivity and satisfaction at work. Before accepting a position, it is crucial to research the culture of a company or employer to see if it is a good fit for you. Many companies have probationary periods for new employees so both the employee and the employer can better predict the long-term outcome. Such trial periods can identify a relationship that isn't workable or one that creates a win-win situation. You are more likely to develop good relationships with your co-workers if your goals and work ethic are similar. You simply can't project how a job will evolve until you test the waters on your first few projects.

Some work-mates develop a deep friendship that lasts long after they leave that workplace. The challenging aspect of work-related relationships is that we often have little say in choosing them. Sometimes, the best we can do with incompatible co-workers is simply to accept them as they are and learn to give them a wide berth. On the flip side, we will surely recognize and celebrate our relationships with like-minded people we encounter in our jobs. Collaboration and successful projects will bloom with these work-mates.

Collaborative relationships within a business contribute to its success. I would go so far as to say that the energy in a workplace is one of the most important aspects of a business. Robin, our neighborhood café owner, is extremely successful because she has created an inviting, warm atmosphere, in addition to serving delicious coffee drinks and food. She hires people who reflect this spirit. She and her employees greet customers with a helpful attitude. She expects them to leave their personal drama at the door when they arrive at work and makes it clear they are not to complain or discuss their personal lives at length. She encourages a relaxed repartee among her workers as well, so they can enjoy their work hours together. The positive energy of her café enhances her success.

You've probably recognized (perhaps subconsciously) both positive and negative vibrations emanating from the business establishments you patronize as well as from the employees who work there. You can choose where to spend your time and money. Which places and people beckon you to return? I choose to shop where I feel welcome when I walk through the door.

The same is true in my own work environment. I once told my employee Janette that I had only one hard and fast rule in my company. Her shoulders tensed as she anticipated a rigid guideline. We both dissolved into laughter when I told her, "If it isn't fun, we won't do it!" I aspire to adhere to this principle when making business and hiring decisions.

Moving Free Mantras for Relationships

These principles of moving free—acceptance, truth, empathy, forgiveness, laughter, collaboration, self-care, and self-reliance—are cornerstones of relationships that will enhance both your personal and professional interactions.

Moving Free

> I accept myself as I am at this moment.
> I agree to accept you exactly as you are.
> I hope you will accept me as I am, as well.

I discussed the importance of "accepting what is" in Trail Marker One. This applies to accepting yourself as you are as well as accepting others as they are. When you accept yourself exactly as you are, where you are, right here, right now, you will learn to love yourself. You will be able to more readily establish healthy relationships with others. Accepting yourself requires being honest with yourself by weighing your good and your not-so-pretty aspects.

Accepting others as they are is a fundamental principle of relationship building that is vital to the success of a healthy friendship or work relationship. You cannot control others any more than you can avoid the unexpected twists and turns in your own life. Expecting others to act the way you want them to in order to fulfill your personal needs is disrespectful and fruitless. It creates frustration for them and for you. When you catch yourself judging or trying to control someone, repeat the above affirmation.

Although the principle of acceptance may be intellectually clear, it isn't always easy to implement. It requires diligent practice. Acceptance reaps the fabulous gift of freedom for yourself and for those you love. As you release unrealistic expectations of others, the weight of the world will be lifted from your shoulders. And moreover, from the shoulders of those you care for. How sweet it is. That's what moving free is all about.

> I will be truthful in all my relationships,
> realizing that a meaningful connection
> cannot exist without truth.

A positive relationship is only possible within the realm of truth. Even when it is uncomfortable, it is important to speak your truth in a loving way, at the appropriate time and place. A meaningful friendship or love relationship is an open one. If you can't be completely transparent, especially with your significant other, there is an elephant in the room.

No two people will agree on everything, but both have a right to speak their truth. Sometimes another's fresh viewpoint sparks personal growth. Or it may lead to the realization that the other person is incapable of being truthful. If that is the case, it may be time to reevaluate whether the relationship is healthy for both parties. If it is not, a bit of processing and even withdrawing from such a relationship might be a reasonable response.

> As I interact with others, I will have empathy for them.
> Only in this way can mutual understanding flourish.

Having empathy and considering another's viewpoint creates a sense of understanding that fosters a strong connection. It is also crucial that you do not take personally everything someone says. Their comments are coming from their particular perspective, based on their past and their current situation. Realize that it's not about you. Choose to filter their remarks with that understanding.

In this age of electronics, it is important to write and read with non-judgment. If you receive a message, note, letter, or e-mail, read it with empathy. In turn, when you create a message using the written word, be sure you are writing it with a positive intent. A conversation or written communication between individuals who can empathize with each other is mutually supportive and satisfying.

It is also wise to encourage give-and-take interactions. If you are thinking only of yourself or the other person is thinking only of him or herself, a dialogue isn't possible. Either way, what might have been a conversation becomes a monologue. Life is not about watching someone onstage or being onstage yourself. Who wants to hear someone go on and on about themselves? When one party makes it all about himself, the other person shuts down. A meaningful conversation based on mutual concern is much more fruitful. Learn to listen with patience, knowing that when it's your turn to express yourself, they will do the same.

> Forgiveness loosens the knots of judgment and anger that bind my spirit, allowing love to flow freely again.

When others fail to meet our expectations or hurt us deeply, we may feel profoundly sad or angry. Those strong feelings may feel like a knot that can't be loosened. Allowing resentments or hurt feelings to separate us jeopardizes the relationship.

We must examine our dark feelings and bring them into the light in order to heal them. We must recognize that every one of us is doing the best we can, given our history and current circumstances. If we both are able to share our perspectives in a non-hurtful way, mutual empathy can be restored. Forgiveness becomes possible. We can release the knots of resentment only by truly forgiving ourselves and others.

Mutual forgiveness liberates us to bond in a new way. But even if the other person doesn't think they have done anything wrong and refuses to apologize, we can still choose to send forgiving and loving vibrations their way. Who knows what positive effect such a mental blessing might reap? Either way, we will be able to move past our own negative feelings. Truly releasing such feelings restores our attention to our intended pathway.

Forgiving my Dad for being so strict and critical during my childhood had been a lifelong challenge for me. Once I left home, I rarely saw him as we both went on with our lives. He remarried three times. I was finally able to deeply forgive him for hurting me during the counseling I pursued to heal my failing marriage. My act of forgiveness freed me to share some enjoyable interactions with my Dad. During a week I spent taking care of him shortly before his passing, he finally told me he had always been proud of me. It was a comforting final encounter that might not have occurred if I hadn't forgiven him ten years earlier.

Laugh out loud!
A few moments of laughter dissolves hours of stress.

Humor is crucial to healthy relationships. Friends, loved ones, and co-workers with whom we can easily laugh are uplifting. It has been scientifically proven that laughter reduces stress and even promotes healing. Allow yourself to discover more reasons to chuckle. Even in the midst of difficult circumstances, opportunities for frivolity arise. Moving free is about embracing laughter as often as possible.

Laughter!

Laugh with others. Laugh at yourself.
Don't store your laughter on a shelf.
Chuckle with your family, chortle with your friends
Whatever else fills up your time, take some time to giggle today.
Just throw your head back and laugh with glee
You'll feel better. Try it and see!

Laughter is healing and bonding. Being able to gently tease someone or make fun of a situation or yourself diffuses tensions and opens the lines of communication. Learning to accept teasing is equally important.

I mentioned earlier the uncontrollable laughter Peggy and I shared during my difficult childhood. Looking back, I can see our giggling fits provided a welcome release of stress and a respite from my troubled home life. To this day, I generously share laughter with my friends. Even during my cancer battle, I enjoyed some humorous moments.

Our friends Ingrid and Scott planned a dinner out with us to celebrate one of my cancer treatment milestones. I excused myself during the meal to use the restroom. I had worn my wig that night and my scalp was feeling itchy, so I took it off to scratch my scalp. At that very moment, the electricity suddenly flickered off. I did my best to replace the wig on my head before returning to our table. The electricity had come back on, and all of a sudden I saw Ingrid rushing toward me. She grabbed me by the arm and guided me back into the bathroom. Amidst peals of laughter, we realized I had put my wig on backwards and it looked ridiculous. Once we had resituated my wig and subdued our giggles, we headed back to the table. What a hilarious opportunity to relieve some accumulated stress!

> Self-reliance is a beautiful thing.
> It is up to me to create the pure joy
> that comes from embracing my own unique journey.

When you find yourself being pushed or bullied by others, repeat this mantra and re-establish your right to be who you are meant to be. No one else can build or destroy your destiny, for it is singularly yours. You came into this world alone and will leave it alone. That is not to say you won't enjoy sharing your life with others. Seeking or giving advice is a valuable aspect of friendship and love. Mutually supportive relationships are true blessings. But in the end, it is surely up to you to follow your heart and create your own fulfillment.

Allowing others to lead you down a path they envision for you is denying your natural power of self-reliance. No one else can recognize the correct crossroads for you. Sometimes it is wise to consult with experts to glean alternatives when you feel lost. Absorb what you can from others, but ultimately trust yourself to recognize when it is time to pursue an alternate route that serves you better. Trust your intuition when it comes to choosing your friends, opportunities, and direction.

Each day in which you *simply know* what choice is best for you and embrace that choice without interference from others, is a bright day indeed. For that day brings you yet another step closer to your journey toward self-reliance.

My sense of self-reliance finally surfaced in our empty nest years. I found my power to insist on fulfilling my life mission of writing. Others thought they had a better idea of what I should do for work or how I should spend my time. But I eventually chose to invest my Social Security income in the writing and editing of this book. And now that I have launched my writing career, I am willing to make any lifestyle adjustments necessary to continue on my chosen path. This is my choice, and nothing and no one will deter me from my goal.

> Collaboration rather than competition keeps our planet spinning round!

A sense of collaboration is crucial to mutually supportive relationships with co-workers, friends, and loved ones. Trying to compete for control in any situation will surely bring drama and discomfort. A sense of collaboration, on the other hand, will enhance the enjoyment of both parties. And most importantly, the end result of collaborative effort will be far more successful and productive.

In order for a collaborative project to evolve, both parties must listen and respect the other person's viewpoint and strengths. We each have our unique talents and passions. When you combine both people's perspective and experience, both can do what they do best. Taking turns in leading a venture often fosters the best outcome.

Collaboration is particularly important in accomplishing work goals. Being a team player in the workplace is crucial to your success. Step back and allow another person to take the lead in their area of expertise. Discuss a direction and give someone space and freedom to do their part. Show your co-workers that you trust them, and receive the same respect in response.

I have experienced both competitive and collaborative working relationships. I must admit that early on, I was the one who wanted to always have it my way. This was especially problematic during my first career at the Pizza Hut corporate office. Once a co-worker and I became annoyed with each other while producing a training manual. Apparently, I was a little too strong in my response to his ideas, because he suddenly blurted out, "That's why I will become a Vice President before you will." (We had both been on the fast track for promotions for several years, so he knew exactly how to strike out at me). In all honesty, he made a valid point. It helped me recognize that I needed to improve my skills in the art of collaboration. That experience opened a whole new world to me.

Now that I am more honest with myself about my strengths and weaknesses, I am more able to pursue my crystal clear mission of writing to encourage other, and leave other aspects of production, such as publishing and sales, to those who are better equipped to handle them.

As part of that quest, through the recommendation of a friend, I discovered Diane, an experienced publishing professional and consultant. I desperately needed someone to pull my scattered elements together into a coherent whole. She liked my book concept and helped me immeasurably by guiding me through the editing process, objectively seeing the big picture and connecting the dots for me. She appreciated my openness to her wise suggestions. We agreed that our goal was to make my writing the best it could be.

I don't believe it was an accident that I found this talented and like-minded woman to guide me. It was yet another synergistic piece of the collaborative puzzle that forwarded my goal to publish this book.

> I intend to spend less time fulfilling
> the expectations of others.
> Instead, I choose to focus on activities
> that lift my own spirit!

It is possible for us to prioritize our time and energy. To learn to say no to others. To begin saying yes to ourselves. Yes to our sense of peace. Yes to time and space for stillness. Yes to our creative urges. Yes to talking and sharing with people who lift us up. Yes to music that soothes our spirit. Yes to watching nature, feeling the sun shining on us, and following our breath.

It's okay for us to take care of ourselves. We need to resist buying into the guilt trip that others may lay on us about being self-absorbed. The truth is, we have more joy and love to share with others if we nurture ourselves first.

> Making time to rejuvenate myself
> will enhance my time with everyone else.

A little time and space away is not only healthy for us; it also enhances our relationships with others. If we are relaxed, we will have more positive energy to offer others. Treat yourself to a massage, a movie, a trip, or whatever relaxes you when you feel the urge. Don't feel guilty about it. All your connections improve when you rejuvenate yourself from time to time.

As a working mother and wife, I had little time to nurture myself during the busy years when we were raising our children. But I did my best to carve out some time for relaxation when it was possible. I would take walks or ride my bicycle to a park and enjoy being outdoors. I would treat myself to a pedicure once in a while. I would enjoy some girlfriend time or a dinner out with Craig to relax and regroup. Even a short time of escape would rejuvenate me so I could return to my family and job with more enthusiasm.

> Today I will remind myself that
> my job is me, your job is you.

When faced with a challenge or decision, we need to research possible solutions, discuss the situation with others, and ask trusted mentors for their advice. But in the final analysis, we must look within to find our own solutions. Listening to what we hear in our heart will reveal the answers that are truly best for us. Following our gut will eventually reveal the best path.

The right answer for you lies within you. If you base your decisions solely on advice from others, you will miss your mark. If you proceed merely to meet the expectations of others, your heart will not be in the game. If you follow your instincts, your answer will come, in your way and in your time. You will simply know. It will feel right. When it does, step out with courage and act with confidence and belief.

It follows that we cannot dictate others' thoughts or actions. We may sometimes want to rescue someone else whom we feel is off course. But we cannot fix anyone else. If we have a strong intuition regarding their situation and if they give us permission to do so, we can offer advice. Otherwise, all we can do is demonstrate our own autonomy and in turn, respect theirs.

During our hike together, Craig couldn't take the steps for me. All he could do was encourage me. It wasn't his job to save me from my fear of pressing on.

✼✼✼

Once we have cleared all the remaining debris, the path ahead looks inviting. As we conquer the steeper path in the forest and see the gentler incline ahead, we can feel the warmth of the sunshine on our faces. Our ascent is exhilarating. We can look back now and appreciate how far we've come.

We have taken the necessary steps toward our growth and freedom by clearing roadblocks and improving our relationships. We can rest and celebrate our progress, realizing that we are at least halfway to the summit. The vistas are much broader and sweeter from this vantage point on the trail. There are so many reasons to celebrate already. We might even do a little happy dance.

Taking the time to re-energize for our continuing ascent toward moving free is crucial to reaching new plateaus of joy. So, stretch out and relax for a bit before you continue on your trek. Bask in the warmth of the sunshine and listen to the sweet singing of the birds. Celebrate this moment of rest. You've earned it.

During the intense counseling that Craig and I pursued in the middle of our marriage, our counselor advised us to take breaks from our tough discussions to simply relax together. I'll never forget one beautiful spring afternoon we shared; we lazed away the afternoon, buying CDs and eating hamburgers at our favorite dive. Neither of us brought up any issues. Together we simply embraced the sunshine, the guilty pleasure of the greasy burgers, and our new music. Reestablishing the ease between us in this way was an important step in rekindling our love for each other.

Repeating the affirmations out loud, considering how they relate to your personal experience, and journaling about them will begin to illuminate your path to moving free. Subtle changes in your sense of freedom and joy might be sinking into your spirit by now as a result of integrating the affirmations, poetry, and guided journaling questions into your life.

☙☙☙

Take some time for self-reflection about your relationships. Examine how you can move more freely in all your relationships by asking yourself these questions:

- *Do I repeat the same self-defeating habits in relationships that result in similar disappointing outcomes? What are these habits?*
- *Am I setting healthy boundaries with others and insisting they adhere to them?*
- *Do I respect others' boundaries? Make note of situations that are problematic or successful in this regard.*
- *Am I constantly disappointed in love? If so, what might I be doing in relationships that continue to result in negative responses from others?*
- *Am I blaming others for my own difficulties in relationships?*
- *Do I spend too much time with negative people out of a sense of obligation? Who should I limit my time with in order to move free in my daily life?*
- *What troubling relationship habits might I relinquish in order to manifest healthier relationships in the future?*
- *What friends, teachers, coaches, and family members have particularly enhanced my life? List these people and take a moment to appreciate their importance in your life.*

Trail Marker Three: Your Quest for Your Intended Life Purpose

Now that you've conquered the rougher terrain below, your renewed energy and determination kick in. You feel prepared to face the challenges ahead, using your newly honed skills to discover your life purpose. You take one last glance downward at the steep path you traversed and look upward toward new horizons, excited about the possibilities of living with a clearer sense of purpose and abundance.

My Trek to My Life Purpose

I have had three distinct careers in my life. With a great deal of pressure to finish college and begin supporting myself following my graduation in the '70s, I did what was expected of me. I immediately looked for a good job with a salary sufficient to sustain me.

I had majored in psychology, but I didn't have the resources to pursue a career in counseling or related job, which would have required a master's degree. I had no idea what I really wanted to do, but I knew I wanted to move to Kansas City, so I researched jobs through friends who were living there. I landed a position with RCA Computer Division as a Systems Engineer. Talk about a huge shift in direction!

After a number of other positions in computer programming, I eventually landed a job at the Pizza Hut headquarters in Wichita, Kansas. This was during a period of explosive growth, when they were opening more than 250 stores each year. The management team was young and enthusiastic—a perfect culture for me. I was promoted four times during my six-year stint with them. It was an exciting journey. I did everything from sitting in a corner programming their payroll system to rolling out their computerized cash register system nationwide. Eventually, I was developing training manuals (my first writing gig), managing their support center for the rollout, and traveling across the country to train regional management personnel. I was able to develop my writing skills and refine my interpersonal communication skills. My professional acumen grew during those hectic years, and I glimpsed possibilities for my later career path.

I was having the time of my life and earning a substantial salary. Craig and I married, and I continued traveling for business. When our son Tyler arrived, I was able to find excellent childcare for him in the home of a large, happy family. However, the birth of our daughter Lauren changed everything. For one thing, the cost of paying childcare for two babies was sobering. And I discovered that working full time with two children under age three was far more demanding than doing the same with only one child.

Shortly after I returned from maternity leave, I realized I simply couldn't keep up with my demanding job and familial obligations. I presented the vice president of our division with a plan to job-share my position with a very capable woman in my department. At the time, flexible hours and job-sharing were new concepts. He made it clear that he didn't want to be the first in the company to "open that can of worms." I finally made the difficult decision to resign from that lucrative and satisfying job.

My choice to stay home with our young children changed our financial circumstances dramatically, but it seemed like the only plausible choice at the time. I enjoyed being a full-time homemaker and mother to our adorable babies for several years. However, I always sensed that this was not my true calling.

The downside of taking a break from my corporate position surfaced several years after leaving Pizza Hut when I tried to reenter the work force in the burgeoning computer industry. I was shocked to learn that I had lost my edge because the technology had changed so dramatically.

As a result, I discovered my next career path as a showroom manager in various gift and apparel marts. This role easily evolved into a career as a sales professional of commercial-grade textiles and furniture. My sense of color, design, fabrication, and fashion served me well in these positions. I had also taken a course in loom weaving and had a working knowledge of textiles.

I created artistic presentations that sparked the interior architects' inclination to specify my fabrics for their projects. I also provided technical content knowledge, a collaborative approach, and excellent follow-up. This job suited my talents and interests, and I was successful in meeting my quotas and satisfying my clients. The financial rewards in this industry weren't as great, but I was able to strike a healthy balance between my maternal role and my career.

It was only after my battle with cancer and when both children were in college that I was able to discover and pursue my third career—writing. I finally feel that I am doing what I was born to do, and I'm loving every minute of it. At long last, I am using my innate talents and passions to pursue my destiny: lifting others up by sharing the lessons of my personal journey of awakening.

Getting Real with Where You Are

Your first step in moving free toward your life purpose is to honestly evaluate your satisfaction with your current career, life, and location. Your life purpose is not necessarily reflected in how you make your living, although it could be. Your life purpose might be volunteering for a non-profit organization or raising your children. Or it could be your high-stakes sales job.

Some fortunate people recognize their life purpose from a young age and progress quickly toward it. Others, like me, take a circuitous path and simply do what they must do to make a living for most or all of their life. If you aren't already doing work that you love, it's time to contemplate a change. Pursuing a certain career because it is lucrative or because someone you know is successful at it will not bring you the life satisfaction that you need in order to flourish. The sooner you find your intended work, the happier and more fulfilled you will be. If you aren't doing what you feel passionate about, this trail marker will help you move in the direction of fulfilling your personal destiny.

> I will frequently ask myself this telling question:
> How do I wish to spend my time?

Answering this all-important question on a regular basis is the key to determining whether you have found your life purpose. Comparing your current situation with your end goal is a productive first step. Whatever career path you have chosen, reevaluate it thoughtfully. Make a list of pros and cons of your current employment, income, and satisfaction level. If money were no object and all your needs were fulfilled, would you continue on your current path or choose another fork in the road? Are you

Moving Free

experiencing the joy of collaborating rather than competing with your co-workers to reach common goals? Are you doing a job that you deeply dislike merely to fulfill your ego's demands for more, more, more material goods? Do you feel valued by your employer?

After evaluating your current status, if you recognize that you can't wait to begin your day because you are passionate about your work, you are fortunate. If you love the work you do, have financial abundance, and feel you are contributing something of value, you are ahead of the game, and you can skim over the next few pages.

On the other hand, if you often dread the day ahead, it's time to face the facts: you may not have found your true calling in life or the right situation in which to move forward with your vision. When you don't feel stimulated or energized by your work, you must reconsider your direction. Perhaps it's time to leave the comfort and security of your safe but dull job with a large company. Or maybe your position has been eliminated because of a downturn in your employer's company and it's time to start your own business. Perhaps you're longing to spend time with your growing children, or, conversely, it's time to move back into a career outside of the home.

Maybe you need to further your education to pursue your desired path, or you want to start your own business but don't have the confidence or funds to embrace that dream. With all the online courses, small business seminars, and public funding opportunities that are available today, you have more choices than ever. In our technically advanced era, you can get the education, guidance, and money you need to start your own company.

Consider both the upside and the downside of the phenomenal change in our economy since the major economic downturn that started in 2008. Corporate downsizing, entrepreneurial trends, and telecommuting opportunities started long before the crash and have changed the face of the American workplace. As a result, you have more flexible options for reinventing your career if you are a victim of the downsizing of a large company or the demise of a smaller one.

For example, some businesses have eliminated or outsourced positions in the areas of marketing and promotions. Even though these functions are crucial to the growth and success of a company, they are often the first to go when a budget crunch occurs. Hiring people on a consulting basis is often the most viable option. My friend Ingrid has been able to procure contracts with several organizations that pay her a monthly retainer, which enables her to make a living in her chosen field from her home office.

Even if working on a consulting basis or becoming an entrepreneur is born out of necessity, it allows people to do their dream work in a less restrictive atmosphere. It also affords them more balance between their work and leisure time. That's one reason entrepreneurship has seen significant growth as an alternative way of generating an income.

The emergence of e-commerce is another opportunity for individuals to market their original ideas and products. Fulfillment companies make it possible to eliminate the up-front costs of manufacturing and distributing your products, inventions, or designs. Essentially, they procure your inventory, warehouse it, and ship your Internet orders and receive a percentage of the income for providing these services. This method allows an individual to start such a business quickly and inexpensively.

Many manufacturers of the best cutting-edge products are choosing to distribute them through network marketing and direct sales. The effectiveness of word-of-mouth advertising and the convenience of ordering online are the cornerstones of these businesses. Becoming a distributor for such companies is proving to be a viable career option. With the current technology and minimal start-up costs, an individual can make a living without the sizeable risks involved in starting a traditional business. Many colleges now offer degrees in network marketing. Young people in particular are becoming financially independent while having more time for family and leisure activities in this way.

Refocusing your life's direction is no small task. Your personal answers will unfold over time. Since gratitude is an important part of your growth, take a moment to celebrate the fact that you have options and the freedom to pursue work that fulfills you.

> I will allow my unique passions and talents
> to emerge within my spirit today.

Some say that we each signed up to be born at a certain time for a certain purpose. Whether you believe that or not, embracing your individuality is your birthright. Your skill and passion could lead you to pursue a career as an executive, entrepreneur, artist, writer, or nurturer of children and others in need. The wide range of talents of all humans are woven together, creating a beautiful tapestry of life.

Finding your place within that tapestry may take time and experimentation. Only you can choose your dream work. You may research potential alternatives for careers that sound appealing to you. It might be beneficial to seek advice from someone who is successful within that arena. But ultimately it is you who must take the steps necessary to transition into work you love.

You must be flexible enough to explore various scenarios, no matter how circuitous that search may become. Dabble in possibilities. Don't remain stuck inside the box of others' rules and restrictions.

You won't be able to force an answer to appear on demand. Given time and trial and error, your destiny will eventually rise into your consciousness, perhaps in the most unexpected way, at the most unexpected time. Your most pressing task is to hold the intention of your dream career within your spirit and be flexible enough to grasp opportunities as they appear.

I am encouraged by the young people of today. Many choose their own way and find ways to earn a living that suits their circumstances. They balance the demands of their lives in true life partner fashion. Sometimes the woman works outside the home and the man becomes Mr. Mom. I smile when I see the young man with his two young children in our neighborhood coffee shop. He is willing and able to be the parent in charge. His children adore him. He is clearly enjoying his important contribution to their upbringing. I often can't resist my urge to say hello and applaud him for his fatherly skills.

Remember that it may take time to find an equilibrium that works for you and your loved ones. My own circuitous career path demonstrates that it takes some of us longer than others to find our true calling in life. It is never too late to pursue your dreams. I was a late bloomer. In light of how deeply I enjoy my current career, my long, winding journey was ever so worth it.

In the Interim

Finding your dream work won't happen overnight. If you want to change careers or are forced to do so, you may very well have to do something in the interim that you think doesn't fit your capabilities. After leaving my successful textiles sales career, I worked several years for my friend Tim, who owned a lovely Asian antique and modern home furnishing shop called Black Bamboo. His partner, Brad, who knew me from my hard-driving sales days, was astonished that I wanted to take this part-time job at entry level pay in a retail store. Brad understandably thought it was a step backward in light of my previous career path. But I was spending time and money on product design and writing, working my way toward making my dream work into a profitable venture. In the meantime, I was earning money in an enjoyable way that was much less demanding on both my time and energy.

I had to accept my current reality. I had chosen to leave my textile sales career. This sales job filled the bill in the meantime so I could make plans for my new business venture. Once I got my own business off the ground, I moved on. But while I worked for Tim, I represented him well and sold many beautiful products to his interesting customers. I simply did my best—which I must say was pretty good—because of my knowledge and passion for interior design and ability to connect with people.

If you have an interim period, utilize your free time by exploring other options or working toward your desired goal. Think outside the box. Seek out fresh possibilities. Remain open to alternatives. Experiment with hobbies and jobs that intrigue you. Take a course that enlightens you. Shadow someone whose career appeals to you. Volunteer or intern in an associated field. Examine your innate talents and passions. When you find something that resonates with you, pursue it further. Take a chance on a different scenario. Doing so will serve you well in the long run.

> I will strive to do my best.
> Then I will simply *let it go*.

Whatever job you are doing—be it born of necessity, fulfillment of your immediate financial needs, or a choice—strive to maintain a positive work ethic. Always give it the best effort you can muster.

If you are planning an event or a project, do it to the best of your ability. Prepare and practice and do whatever it takes to feel and be organized. Set a positive intention for your desired outcome by visualizing it in your mind's eye, as if it were occurring now.

Then simply let it go and resist the urge to second-guess yourself. Don't waste your valuable time obsessing about it. Trust that it will turn out exactly as you imagined it would. Remind yourself that in retrospect, situations usually turn out exactly as they were meant to be. Sometimes surprises arise, but often they are pleasant ones. Even if they aren't so sweet, they may provide valuable pointers for future efforts.

> Rejecting rigidity and embracing elasticity
> is crucial to growth.

Another critical aspect of moving free in the direction of your dream work is releasing any rigid ideas that have hampered your growth thus far. Once again, you must remove the roadblocks you have created through your self-doubts or fear of the unknown. In order to move toward the person you wish to become, you must be flexible enough to recognize and seize opportunities with confidence.

Moving Free

I must admit I was rather rigid during my last textiles sales gig. I represented a gorgeous boutique fabric line at the time, and I had been successful in selling it to my customers. When Brad, the company's national sales manager, moved back to Kansas City, they took the line away from me and gave it to him. This was a logical choice for the manufacturer, but I was deeply disappointed by the loss of my favorite line. When Brad came to pick up the samples, I simply opened our garage door, handed him the boxes, and turned and walked back into the house. This little fit of passive aggressive anger was selfish and rude. I wasn't able to be gracious about the transfer. I would like to think I would handle the situation better if it occurred now. And yes, this was the same Brad who interviewed me for the job at Black Bamboo several years later—talk about having to eat crow! Fortunately, we became friends and are able to laugh about that incident now.

When I was growing up in the '50s and '60s, the career choices for both men and women were more limited than they are now. The majority of men worked for one company their entire life, in order to support their families and secure a pension for their retirement years. Most married women were expected to stay home and raise their children full-time. Career choices for single or widowed women were even more restricted.

My mother-in-law Marilyn once showed my daughter and me a book she had received early in her marriage. My daughter's jaw dropped as she recited excerpts for us. It described the duties of a married mother of that era. It detailed the specifics of preparing for her husband's arrival in the evenings. Her tasks were to make herself presentable with a clean dress and makeup, instruct her children to go play in their rooms, and have a balanced meal ready to place on the table she had meticulously set. When he arrived, she was to greet him with good cheer, bring him his slippers, and serve him an alcoholic beverage (or three). Never, under any circumstances, was she to ask him about his day, because it might disrupt the perfect haven that she had created for him. It was all there in black and white.

Despite rigid societal norms and expectations of their eras, there have always been and will always be free spirits who follow their passions and pursue the lives of their dreams. Amelia Earhart and Julia Child were women who embraced their freedom and talents. Ernest Hemingway and Pablo Picasso lived their own dream lifestyles. Both male and female artists, writers, and actors pursued their passions with gusto. They were undaunted by the naysayers who judged them.

The shift in our society's attitude toward workplace roles in the last fifty years is nothing short of phenomenal. Both men and women are choosing their careers based on their particular talents and passions. Entrepreneurs are flourishing because they have stepped outside the corporate box, choosing to do their own thing. Creative individuals who produce today's books, art, music, and movies are plentiful and prolific. Women are rising to the pinnacle of business and politics because they are capable and free to embrace their desired career paths.

Whether you are young and searching for your first career or older and pursuing your second or third career as I did, allow your heart to guide you and your passions and talents to illuminate your path. Celebrate the expanded opportunities available today to fulfill your own destiny, and remain flexible as you explore your future.

Navigating Your New Path

When you choose a new profession, remember that stepping out in a different direction is a process. Remain open to possibilities and opportunities that arise. Find someone—your life partner, a family member, or friend—who supports your growth. Return the favor by nurturing them and celebrating their chosen lifestyle and work.

> Once I have discovered my passion,
> I will move freely in the direction of my dream work,
> trusting in my synergy.

Once you have identified an exciting new career or job, create a mental picture of yourself doing work you love in that situation. You may wish to draw up a broad plan showing how you might achieve your goal. Or create a vision board of your desired outcome. Do not expect to dictate the exact details—the who, what, when, and how of the matter. Focus on your desired goals and listen to your still voice within. Take concrete steps every week to move your intention forward. Be vigilant for serendipitous situations that might emerge. The right people, the financial means, and the opportunities will appear—unless you block them with a rigid plan or arbitrary deadline.

Be courageous and optimistic as you take each step on your newly chosen path. Trust that stepping outside of your comfort zone will provide positive pointers to your next venture. Heed your inner sense of direction as you walk through open doors with integrity and intention. Remember that living your passion is a journey. Sometimes you may feel as if you are taking one step forward and two steps back, but remember that each step brings you closer to what you intend to do. At every juncture, ask yourself: Am I doing work that I love and loving the work that I do? Respond to this crucial, life-changing question with brutal honesty. Continuing to fool yourself about something that is so important to your happiness and income is counter-productive. Awakening to your full potential and joy is worth some twists and turns, don't you think?

After feeling frustrated for many years while working for others in jobs she didn't enjoy, our daughter-in-law Stefanie created a niche for herself as a free-lance specialist in social media and marketing. Her clients are widespread. She works from the comfort of her home—often with a cat purring on her lap. She connects with her clients in person at industry expos. This new venture utilizes her considerable creative talents and writing skills. She has also experienced a moderate increase in her income. Nice.

> I will simplify my life and my space—
> freeing myself for lightness and growth.

Any time you prepare to make a big shift in your job or career, you must clear the trail ahead before you can proceed. The only way to hike in a forward motion is by simplifying your life.

Transitioning into a new work life involves letting go of old possessions and habits, clearing space for growth. Get rid of those things that no longer serve you. Sell them or give them to someone who has need of them. Don't spend your valuable time moving or storing things you never use. Each time you open a cluttered closet, your energy takes a big downturn. Dive in and de-clutter. It's very important also to squelch your urge to buy things you don't need that crowd your home, office, and mind. This rigorous physical spring-cleaning will also release energy, creating more time and space for moving free.

My longtime friend Kelli introduced me to the importance of simplicity in my life by modeling that principle in her life and career. She lives her belief that in order to make room for new opportunities, we must first release things, people, and situations that no longer serve us as we evolve in our awareness and presence.

Simplifying my life has become a gratifying priority for me, and I have given away and sold many of my belongings in order to create simpler living and working spaces. I've organized my remaining belongings so I can easily find what I need. I've also eliminated activities that drained my energy rather than enhanced it. As a result of embracing this lesson, I have far more time and energy to spend with people and work that lift my spirit and promote my sense of joy and purpose.

Be patient with yourself during your quest for your ideal career. Remember that every job you ever did or are doing enhances your wisdom and self-awareness. Even though you may encounter some detours on the trail toward your desired dream work, as you near the summit of your career path, you will find satisfaction in the journey itself.

ଔଔଔ

- *If you feel you are lacking direction in your career path, begin with a simple exploration of your resources. What are your gifts? Do you naturally excel at certain things? List those skills. Are you utilizing those as a hobby or in your work?*
- *Ask yourself what you truly desire in life. How do you want to spend your time? Don't judge. Just write.*
- *If money were no object, where would you live and what would you do for a living?*
- *If you have found your dream work, express your gratitude for it now.*

Trail Marker Four: When Storm Clouds Gather

Just as we are making progress on our intended journey, storm clouds gather and the rain starts to fall; the thunder booms and the lightning flashes. We have to run for cover and huddle under a tree in our ponchos. We have no choice but to wait out the storm before we are able to resume our hike. We feel frightened and vulnerable. We may be frustrated by the interruption in our forward progress, but we are forced to stop in our tracks.

When exhaustion sets in or darkness descends upon us, how do we keep on trekking? No one escapes adversity in his or her life—no one. Adversity comes in many forms, and we all must deal with it sooner or later. Whether it presents itself in the form of sudden tragedy, serious illness, depression, divorce, anxiety, addiction, financial difficulties, or personal loss matters not. Standing up and walking through it requires courage and stamina and hope.

Traversing the Tough Bends in My Path

The darkest storms in my life were my mid-marriage struggles, my mother's difficult death, and my cancer diagnosis. Each of these challenges seemed overwhelming at the time. There were many days when I awoke in a state of abject terror or deep despair. Some days all I could do was take one frightened step after another.

I was fortunate to have friends and family members who came alongside me to lend a supportive hand during those dark periods of my life. Having been a strong and determined woman for most of my adult life, becoming vulnerable enough to ask for and graciously accept help was one of my most difficult hurdles. I was broken down and had no choice. I had to reach out for the life preserver that was thrown my way, grab onto it, and hold on for dear life. That being said, this was my singular journey. It was up to me to embrace these challenges and allow myself to be transformed in positive ways by them.

My first and most devastating crisis was my separation from Craig. Although I was aware we had been drifting apart for several years, I was shocked when he announced to me that he wanted a separation. It was November of 1992. Tyler was 13 and Lauren was 11. Craig said he wasn't sure he wanted to be married to me anymore.

During those first few weeks he was gone, I couldn't eat and couldn't sleep; I lost weight and felt exhausted. It was fortunate that I had a full-time job at the time, because I could occasionally forget my troubles when I was engaged at work. I told my workmates we had separated, but I vowed to focus on my job and not discuss it during work hours.

When I came home each day, I spent most of my time curled up in the corner of the sofa in the family room, feeling defeated and terrified. I struggled to perform my domestic and parental tasks as best I could, but I was simply going through the motions.

Both children were surprised and upset about the separation, but they felt reassured that they could call and spend time with their dad often. He sometimes took them to his apartment, but we soon settled into a routine at our house that worked better for the kids. When he arrived on Sundays, I either left or went back to the bedroom and shut the door. To help the children cope with the situation, we took them out to dinner together occasionally. These dinners were pleasant and comforting to the kids and to me. Parenting was something Craig and I shared well together, even in these circumstances.

From day one, Craig and I agreed to not criticize each other to the children or discuss our problems with them. Fixing our marriage or ending it was our problem, not theirs. We both took the high road by continuing to put our roles as parents ahead of our struggles. Attending family get-togethers after the children's soccer and basketball games was particularly difficult for me, because I feared that our life together might soon be over.

Paying close attention to the children was crucial to their sense of security. It also provided a healthy coping mechanism for me. Tyler was in junior high and old enough to have activities and friendships that occupied much of his leisure time. He was obsessed with the idea of taking guitar lessons, so I took him to buy his first guitar. This opened a whole new world to him and led him to form a garage band that he would enjoy for years. Lauren was home most of the time. She played with friends and even had some sleepovers, but we still spent a great deal of time together. I remember renting lots of movies on the weekends, so we would have an activity together—one that allowed me to cocoon on the sofa.

My initial reaction to our situation was this: I needed to fix this dreadful circumstance *right now*. After all, I had successfully controlled everything in my life for years, hadn't I? But the universe had other plans for me. It turned out that my need to be in control was the very issue Craig had been struggling with. He said I made him feel as if he couldn't do anything right, so he gradually withdrew from me and gave up trying to help with the household chores and parenting.

It was time for me to regroup. I joined a Bible study group for support and guidance. I bought self-help books and began individual counseling as well as marriage counseling with Craig. I was truly perplexed when my therapist told me there was no quick fix for this terrifying situation. That was a bitter pill for me to swallow.

She suggested I needed to learn to love myself before I could attempt to save our marriage. The first step would be to nurture myself. She helped me realize that I had been so overwhelmed with the business of being a wife, mother, and career woman that I had lost myself somewhere along the way. In the midst of caring for others and focusing on my career, I had been ignoring my own needs.

At first I wondered how I could slow down from this mad life we had created. But eventually I accepted that this was an unfolding journey that Craig and I must take either together or separately.

When I began enjoying the reading and counseling, I knew I was on the path to my emotional recovery. I had always been fascinated with psychology, spirituality, and what made people tick, so my own journey of self-rediscovery was gratifying. I would type uplifting sayings and scriptures and tape them to my vanity mirror. I would repeat these encouragements out loud to myself in the morning to bolster my courage to face that day.

My Blossoming Courage

I curled up in the womb of our sofa,
pulling my wedding ring quilt tightly round me
to warm the abject cold that gripped my soul.

Questions unanswered rattled in my head.
Hadn't I done what was expected?
Hadn't I been the perfect, pretty girl he wanted me to be?
Hadn't I made our home a haven of peace?

Mid-of-night sweats and terrors
ripped my beliefs to shreds.
Who *would* I, who *could* I be,
outside this expected guise?

How could I face their teenage angst?
Be the mom I had so craved myself
help them feel both safe and free
when I was barely breathing?

I pictured my frightened little woman-child
climbing into my Pappy's lap.
"Help me," I pleaded,
desperate to feel his glowing warmth.

I repeated my pitiful promise out loud to myself:
I turn it over. I turn it over. I turn it over!
Tears of fear streaming down my cheeks,
the tiniest glimmer of self-trust was born.

Perhaps I could do this; dredge up the courage
to excavate my long buried brave self.
Maybe I could glimpse my essence again—
that Aries fire that had fizzled so.

Finally, the powerful words on a page resonated.
Right there in print, it called out to me:
"You must unlatch the door of the cage."
A tiny ember sparked within my shrunken belly.

Our nest of unmet expectations was disintegrating, was it not?
Dare I set that balking bird free?
My flames of belief grew more fiery and fierce,
fanning my resolve to step out in courage.

At long last, I spoke it aloud to him.
"I get it now. It's time for you to go.
I'm releasing you to start your life anew."

A warm bubbling confidence, a renewed sense of calm,
slowly settled into my gut like a lazy lava flow.
My resolve finally broke free from the rich loam of hope.
Its strong stem reached skyward
and blossomed fully into the vivid colors of fire.

Through counseling, study, and self-reflection, I had experienced a dramatic shift. My goal now was to embrace a journey of self-discovery and to learn to love myself, regardless of what the future held. I had reached a major turning point, which enabled me to truly set Craig free. At long last, I was ready to accept either outcome—reconciliation or divorce.

I told him that I realized he was no longer committed to me, and I gave him my blessing to start his new life without me. But rather than being the downfall of our relationship, my new confidence liberated his desire to create a fresh start. He recognized that I was truly ready to move on by myself. It was time to decide. He said he enjoyed the peaceful home I had created during his absence, and he wanted to rebuild our marriage. As a result, we began to share some hard truth-telling discussions and tough counseling together.

Healing a relationship requires self-examination and growth by both parties. The fault seldom lies completely with one or the other partner. We were ready to explore each other's perspective about how our relationship had disappointed each of us.

For him, my need to be right and be in control of our life, home, and children was the root of our problems. This came as a complete surprise to me. Clearly, I had work to do on myself to relinquish my need for perfection and encourage him to participate without criticizing him.

My take on our relationship was quite different. When we had a disagreement, it seemed to me he simply froze me out. After a sufficient amount of time had passed, he wanted to proceed as if nothing had happened. This left me frustrated and feeling totally alone. I didn't feel supported or appreciated.

Why hadn't he ever confronted me about these issues? In a counseling session, it became apparent that he had been afraid to. He thought my response would be to lash out in anger. His counselor triggered a shift by asking one simple question: "What have you got to lose?" This helped Craig summon up the courage to honestly express his concerns to me. I told him I had no idea he felt this way and was willing to do what I could to improve our relationship.

We needed to learn how to constructively discuss our issues rather than resorting to anger or complete withdrawal. We had to learn to fight fairly. We had to reveal our feelings honestly and listen with empathy to each other. During this process, we both felt liberated to speak our own truths and openly consider each other's perspective.

Neither of us had seen a healthy model of marriage during our childhoods. His parents lived fairly separate lives (his dad was a traveling salesman), and my parents had had a tumultuous marriage that ended in divorce. Now we could see new possibilities. As we reached out for help, we became committed to rebuilding our marriage into a healthy relationship in which we both felt valued and appreciated.

During our therapy, we were encouraged to relive our early days of meeting and falling in love. We both recounted what originally attracted us to the other. Besides the obvious physical attraction I felt, I was drawn to his child-like enthusiasm and laid-back nature (the opposite of my dad's volatile one). Recalling the joy of falling in love was very important to rekindling our attraction and love for each other.

Our separation had a happy ending. Craig and I both chose to grow and learn through our experience and counseling. I must admit that by the time he was finally ready to recommit, I was on the verge of moving on. However, raising our children together during their crucial teenage years was a strong motivation for both of us. So I decided to let it unfold, knowing I could change my mind after they were on their own.

Instead, our respect, attraction, and love for each other grew. We learned to honestly share our feelings rather than allowing small resentments to create a wall between us. We also learned to laugh together again. What a joy that was and continues to be. Most importantly, we both chose to forgive each other for hurtful actions and disappointments and use what we had learned to recreate our relationship. As a result, we successfully reignited our love and rebuilt our marriage.

We had walked through the fire separately, and now we were walking hand-in-hand. We finally became *life partners*. It was a difficult storm to weather, but we both experienced growth as individuals and as a family by utilizing our newfound relationship skills. It didn't happen overnight, but our family became stronger and happier over the years. We are both grateful to be together and are enjoying our empty nest. The silver linings of our separation are numerous.

It is clear to me that this frightening period of my life provided the opportunity to recreate myself as a stronger, more loving woman. It was a gigantic step toward moving free. Once you have traversed such adversity, you have a renewed gratitude for your life and love for yourself and your spouse. I had a renewed confidence in myself and found more joy in sharing the simple things with Craig. Before we were separated, I was often annoyed that he chose to spend Sunday afternoon watching football rather than spending time with me. After our reconciliation, I enjoyed watching football with him, napping, or reading. Just being together in our peaceful space was comforting and relaxing.

My next momentous wake-up call came shortly after Craig and I had rekindled our love. My mother's cancer and her long and painful dying process were very difficult for all of us. There is no doubt that witnessing my mother's end-of-life suffering and hearing her revelation ("I must move free") was the single greatest synchronicity of my lifetime. My takeaway from this sad period is that we each have a choice whether to remain stuck or to move free in our life. Embracing the seemingly random events that mold our lives is surely one of the greatest secrets of moving free. My pathway to personal liberation was long and difficult, but oh-so-worth the tough trek.

I came to the next gigantic bend in my path—my breast cancer diagnosis—two years after my mother's passing. How could this be? I had been religious about getting yearly mammograms since I turned forty and had tried to live a healthier life style. But during a regular self-exam, I felt a lump and immediately knew what it was. My mammogram confirmed my suspicions.

Apparently I had more lessons to learn before I could fulfill my destiny of moving free. Specifically, I had to turn my treatment over to my doctors and nurses, my duties over to my coworkers, and my courage over to my Spiritual Source.

Recounting war stories from my cancer battle isn't my thing. As part of letting go of the past and living in the present, I have gradually released the tough memories of my treatment and reconstruction surgery. But to give you an indication of the intensity and duration of my battle, in a 2½-year period, I had five surgeries and chemotherapy. My initial treatment was completed in 1999. I worked as much as possible during that time and returned to work full-time in 2000. I chose to delay my reconstruction surgery until early in 2001 in order to get back to my job and to regain my health and energy prior to that final procedure.

Again, I drew much of my hope from Scripture and inspirational and self-help books to find encouragement for the tough battle ahead. As I had done during my earlier struggles, I typed encouraging words and affirmations and posted them on my vanity mirror. I repeated them aloud to myself each morning to bolster my resolve to face another frightening day.

Craig truly stepped up to support me during my cancer battle. I soon began referring to him as "my rock." One of his most wonderful gifts of love was taking me on excursions on summer evenings. He would pick me up after work, and we would take long drives out to the horse ranches south of Kansas City. I was having a rough time with my chemotherapy. The fresh air and the sight of horses grazing peacefully in the meadows soothed my waves of nausea. Those outings were the best medicine ever!

Our children couldn't have been more loving and supportive of me. They were terrified that I would die of the same disease that had taken their grandmother, but Craig and I reassured them with our shared belief that I would survive. They were so sweet in their quiet encouragement and consideration for me during that dark period.

Our friends and extended family came to our aid by sitting with Craig during my surgeries, bringing meals for our family, and offering moral support, phone calls, emails, cards, and flowers. One beautiful spring day Pat and Diane took me to a nursery to buy flowers and then planted them in pots for me as I sat and watched on our sunny back patio. Ingrid and Scott planned a weekend trip to the Ozarks to celebrate the completion of my chemotherapy. My longtime friend Marva cared for me during my mastectomy and reconstruction surgeries. Kelli made house calls to adjust my spine. Paula dropped by and ran errands and brought nutritious meals for months following my treatment. She formed a walking team and raised almost $100,000 for Komen for the Cure and Avon in the years that followed, in honor of me and many other women in her life who had battled breast cancer. Talk about supporters who go the extra mile!

As outrageous as it sounds, I consider my cancer to be a great gift because it provided yet another impetus to embrace my free spirit within and to begin moving free every exquisite day. It also forced me to make nutrition and lifestyle changes that have served me well. Even though this was the most serious and life-threatening skirmish of my life, I was able to navigate it with hope and courage because of all I had learned during my other two major wake-up calls.

Following my cancer battle, I began mentoring other women facing cancer and writing affirmations to encourage them. The inspirations I had found and posted on my mirror had helped me traverse my struggles. I wanted to empower others with my creations.

I have come to believe that nothing that happens in our lives is an accident. If we tune in to our inner wisdom and listen to the still voice within as synchronicities appear, our paths will be illuminated with hope, happiness, and love. Exponential personal growth and joy will light our paths, and we will in turn hold up the light for those with whom we share our journeys.

Mantras for Dealing with Adversity

Regardless of the type of challenges we face, we need to bolster our courage in order to navigate a demanding path. The following mantras will strengthen your resolve to persevere.

> I choose to enter the tunnel with hope,
> courageous step by courageous step,
> trusting in the God-light ahead.

Whatever daunting challenges we face, we must grasp every bit of resolve we can conjure up in order to take the next steps. We must focus on each step or task as we navigate through our dark tunnels. There is no way around them.

I'll never forget the morning of my mastectomy surgery. I awoke in a panic, realizing that I would never be the same after that day. Although I was sure having this surgery was the right decision—perhaps a life-saving one for me—I couldn't shake my fright. I uttered some urgent prayers and simply got up and got dressed. It was no doubt one of the most courageous acts of my life. I had to enter that tunnel of treatment with resolve and hope—there was no detour around it. So I forced myself to take each brave step, trusting that I would glimpse the light at the end of it in due time.

When my Aunt Jeanne was diagnosed with ovarian cancer, I shared this affirmation with her. Sadly, her cancer wasn't diagnosed soon enough, so she chose to spend her final days with her family rather than enduring heroic treatments. This affirmation spoke to her as she faced her mortality and the next journey of her spirit. She asked me to repeat it with her, and it gave her great hope that the light at the end of her tunnel would lead to her joyful reunion with her departed loved ones.

> Simply being with nature
> opens my heart to healing.

Once we walk out of our emotional tunnel and into the light, it is important to allow ourselves time to rest and rejuvenate. Recuperation is vital before moving forward.

A few moments of rest might stop that seemingly endless record of to-dos and worrisome thoughts that play in your head. It's a good time to get outside and be alone and still. Breathe. Soothe your spirit. Observing nature will center you. If you can't go outside, simply close your eyes and travel in your mind to a destination that feeds your spirit. Feel the warmth of the sun. Hear the roar of the waves or the wind in the trees. Feel the warm touch of Spirit. Be thankful for the healing place available within your inner space. You are safe there. Feel better? Feel lighter?

For me, relaxing in nature has always been soothing and healing. Following my treatment, gardening was a wonderful way for me to relax and renew myself. I spent many hours watering and pruning my plants. Sometimes, I just closed my eyes and listened to the chirping of the birds in our backyard. Healing my body and spirit in this way prepared me for my new reality as a cancer survivor.

> I choose to *be resilient*.
> When a tough patch has passed, I will move free from it.
> I will consciously shift my focus back to joy.

You must also choose to be resilient in order to return to center. Making an active choice to come back to what's important is a critical part of moving free. Being resilient means not getting stuck in negative emotions. Certainly you can experience and honor the difficult situation. Have a good cry if it's called for. But will it serve you to wallow in sadness? Absolutely not. When the immediate challenge has passed, consciously shift your attention back to your lighter side. In this way, you will feel renewed and ready to be present with the next tough bend in your path, or—even better—new opportunities for joy.

When I am faced with a difficult circumstance, I give my full attention to doing what I can to resolve it. This might mean being present with a friend who is in need of my support, doing what I can to alleviate their pain. Or it might require simply being persistent in solving a pesky problem with technology or finances.

> *I am glowing* with health, vitality, creativity, light, and love.

We all encounter daunting storms, tunnels, and difficulties—that's life. It's not always easy to bounce back from sad or painful interludes. We may feel depleted afterwards. In order to resume living fully, we must first convince ourselves that we can reclaim our joy, laughter, focus, and confidence. Repeating this affirmation aloud sets a positive intention for our future.

Your individual energies work in concert to create your particular glow. Your health and vitality are dependent upon your nutrition as well as your patterns of activity and sleep. When you feel good physically, you have more energy to pursue interests and people who lift your spirits, which sparks your creativity and light. When you love yourself and others, your inner light shines forth.

Imagine tapping into the most powerful, loving, healthy version of yourself. Envision yourself glowing with vitality, creativity, light, and love. You can picture it in your mind's eye. You can activate it. You can enliven your home and your work and your town and your country and your world. Yes, you can.

I traversed a particularly rough road during the six months between selling our old home and settling into our new one. We were virtually vagabonds. I didn't have easy access to the activities, people, exercise, and nutrition that are vital to my wellbeing. I had underestimated the toll this huge life shift would take on my mind, body, and spirit. It left me exhausted and depressed. Once we settled into our home, I was able to nest and rest deeply. And voilá—this affirmation came to me. Meditating upon it every morning restored my natural vitality and joy. I got my glow back!

> I intend to allow the turbulent waters of my life
> to smooth my rough edges.

A beach rock tossed about by the crashing waves gradually becomes rounder and smoother. Similarly, the adversity in our lives might end up smoothing our rough edges a bit. We may feel pretty beaten up after being tossed in unexpected directions. But the relief we feel after the crashing of the waves recedes puts things in perspective. We may take some time to be still and contemplate how certain patterns of thinking have deterred us from going with the natural ebb and flow of our life. After we traverse difficulties and take time for self-reflection, our quest for fulfillment and joy may accelerate. And we might become a light for others as we share our gratitude and joy.

My new perspective opened the gates for my mission in life—to lift up others with the lessons I learned during my most difficult years. You never know when the seemingly random challenges you face might turn out to be *positively life changing.*

> Day by day, I'll embrace my journey—all of it!
> I'll wade through the tough stuff, celebrate the good stuff,
> and *lean into* my own true trek.

When the winds of adversity blow into our lives, the best we can do is to lean into them, pressing courageously forward through the storm. Once the winds have died down, we can focus on our forward progress once again. We must be careful not to allow our adversities to define us or waylay us any longer than is necessary. Shifting our attention and energy back to our intended path, rather than remaining stuck, is crucial.

Caregivers for loved ones who are gravely ill face especially tough challenges, sometimes for many months or years. Once their friend or mate has passed on, they will be stunned and exhausted. It will take some time and effort to heal from that trauma before they are able to move forward with their lives.

When our hearts remain open, we are able to unearth valuable lessons from difficult experiences. We must take time to absorb them. Retaining such wisdom will help us appreciate our health and life and will strengthen our resolve to live our lives to the fullest.

When the good stuff suddenly appears, we need to embrace it and take time to celebrate it. If we allow the good energy to soak into our spirits, feelings of elation will renew us. We'll bask in the glow. Enjoy the ride. Feel the joy. Our renewed resilience will kick in, allowing us to redirect our energy toward the life of our dreams. Yes—now we're back on the trail to moving free.

Once the storm has passed, we are able to stash our ponchos and emerge from our shelter. The smell of the rain-washed pines wafts through the air. The damp wildflowers are brighter after their rain-bath. We are free to proceed on our hike with a renewed appreciation for the sights and sounds of the trail. We are reenergized and confident that we can reach our final destination before sunset, even with this rain delay. We feel as if we have a fresh start as we confidently don our backpacks and forge ahead to the summit that is coming into sight.

CBCBCB

- *What challenges have you faced that stopped you in your tracks? Record how that pain or loss felt. Then try to excavate the lessons you learned and the personal growth you experienced as a result of traversing that difficult journey.*
- *What circumstances brought abject terror into your life? In retrospect, can you see the gifts that arose from the ashes of that experience? Express your gratitude for these gifts. Appreciate how far you have come in your emancipation from difficulties.*
- *How have your rough edges been smoothed over time? What qualities, such as gratitude, resilience, and empathy for others, have you developed as a result of traversing tough times?*

Trail Marker Five: The Simplest Little Meditation Guide Ever!

When I first explored the art of meditation, I read a book that laid out specific rules and timing. I gave it my best shot but found it to be too restrictive and structured for me. Adhering to the required duration (at least an hour) was especially frustrating. The following is a gentler introduction to meditation than those you might have explored before. It is a simple framework for meditating designed to help you get started.

The benefits of meditating are plentiful. Consider the reasons that sound compelling to you before you begin. Over time, your particular goals for your meditation practice will change and evolve.

Why Should I Meditate?

Meditating enables you to:

- calm your mind, body, and spirit
- reduce stress, anxiety, or depression
- distract and redirect addictive urges
- clear the nagging, negative, and repetitive thoughts that clutter your mind
- calm your fears
- access your inner voice (whatever you may call it: intuition, your angels, spirit guides, or the Holy Spirit)
- focus on your tasks at hand
- discover specific solutions for your dilemmas
- boost your creativity
- envision future possibilities
- reconnect with your gratitude and joy

- set a positive intention for your day or for an interaction
- illuminate your path

> Today I'll visit that peaceful space within my heart made for dealing, healing, and illuminating my path!

When you feel sad or confused or anxious, getting in touch with the peaceful space within your heart will soothe you. Being still, breathing, and clearing your mind of repetitive, annoying thoughts will free you. We sometimes experience adversity, depression, anxiety, or confusion. The silver lining of our difficulties is the life lessons and growth they impart. Meditating gives us pause, allowing us to just *be* so that we can become more open to those lessons and that growth.

My greatest aha-moments often came following my toughest challenges. When I looked back, I realized that my storms—such as my cancer battle—were exquisite gifts—ones that propelled me toward my destiny. Meditation allowed me the time and space to reflect.

Reconnecting with your very own internal guidance system in order to illuminate your path is the icing on the cake. Stepping back from the business of everyday living allows time to deal with and heal from trials and reflect upon your current relationships, work, and life direction. It also frees your spirit to explore exciting new possibilities. So let's get started!

Preparing to Meditate

Choose a space: Your meditation space should be private and quiet. It should be pleasing to your senses—indoors or outdoors, warm or cool. It helps if it is uncluttered, with a comfortable place to sit or lie down. Preferably, the lighting and windows will be such that the area can be made fairly dark. You may also wish to play soothing music or white noise. Inform others in the house that you need privacy for a while and close the door, if possible.

Choose a mantra that resonates with you: For rhythm, the mantras should consist of a pair of two- to three-word phrases. The following are some examples that appeal to me: I am safe / I am free. I am safe / I am well. I am / who I am. I love / I am loved. I trust / I have hope. I have joy / I am free. I am safe / I choose joy. All is well / I move free. You get the idea. You may initially try some of these and choose one or make up others that fit your desire for safety, freedom, health, joy, or whatever you need right now.

Leave your worries at the door: Your goal is to clear your mind of whatever challenges or pressing "to dos" you are facing. Doing so will create the inner space necessary for new ideas and inspirations to rise into your consciousness. Before you enter your sacred space, pause and picture yourself gently circling your hand around your head, scooping up any repetitive thoughts, and securing them in your closed fist. Next, stash them in a real or imagined box with a lid just outside your meditation space. You could pick them up on your way out if you wish to, but I'm betting you won't want to.

Get comfortable in your special place: I sometimes lie on my back on the bed with my knees bent (feet resting on the mattress and the back of my neck supported). Or I lie down in a fetal position on my right side. Or I recline in a comfortable chair and ottoman (with my knees slightly elevated) or in a recliner, with a soft throw over me. For those who practice yoga, the traditional cross-legged seated position might feel natural. You will establish your own comfortable positions and change them as needed.

Engage in a mental journey to a physical place that feels uplifting to you: If you love the beach, try to feel the warmth of the sun on your face and hear the gentle crashing of the waves. If you love the mountains, envision yourself in the woods and listen to the birds singing and the babbling brook beside your trail. I sometimes practice this part of meditation when I'm in the dentist's chair in order to take my mind off the procedure.

Meditate

- *Close your eyes and mouth.*
- *Breathe in* deeply through your nose. Envision your lungs filling with oxygen and expanding. Hold the air in for a moment.
- *Breathe out* slowly through your nose. Observe the air flowing out and your lungs contracting. Hold for a moment. You may wish to lower your chin slightly and listen to the sound created by doing so.
- *Repeat.* Follow your breath with your mind, focusing on the in-breath and the out-breath.
- Add your mantra, as follows:
- *Silently repeat the first line of your mantra as you breathe in. Hold.*
- *Silently repeat the second line of your mantra as you breathe out. Hold.*
- *Repeat this breath/mantra exercise for as long as you feel comfortable doing so.*
- Your goal is to stay focused on your breath and your words. When thoughts distract you, simply begin again. Gently breathe out the thoughts and refocus on your mantra. You can deal with those pesky tasks and responsibilities later. This is your time for quiet reflection.

- You may also want to scan your body from the top to the bottom, searching for areas of tension or discomfort. Consciously breathe into those areas. Feel the warmth of relaxation moving through you. You might wish to envision a column of sparkling, soothing light descending down over you. Observe this warming light as it slowly moves downward through your body. Imagine it is melting your stress and pushing it away. Observe the tension flowing out the bottom of your feet and sinking into the earth below.
- *Listen to your still voice within.* Heed any clear thoughts or directions that come to you as you continue to follow your breath.
- *Stop when you sense that you are finished.*
- *Gently open your eyes and stretch your body.*
- *Slowly rise and quietly leave your special space.* In order to preserve this renewed sense of tranquility, you'll resist any urge to pick up the worries you stashed in the box, right?
- *Make note of any positive ideas or solutions* that came to you during your time of reflection. Although you may not receive such messages initially, they will start coming to you as you progress into an easy, natural meditation practice.

> That's it. Keep it simple.
> *Make it your own.*

As you practice meditation, your personal style will emerge. You will have preferences for where and when you meditate. You might wish to have particular items in the space, or you may want to do a walking meditation outdoors. Embrace whatever seems natural to you. Eventually, it will flow naturally, providing tranquility and redirection for your ascending journey.

Although it initially took some practice, I now effortlessly awaken in the morning in a meditative state. Words that inspire my writing and clear instructions for specific tasks flow into my consciousness. I keep my tablet at my bedside so I can immediately record them before they float away. It sounds crazy, but that's how simply and naturally my inspiration and practical directions come. I never know what thoughts will arise, but I have learned that trusting and acting upon them enables me to reap significant results.

You may wish to emulate my example by journaling the messages you receive during your meditations. Be courageous in allowing these revelations to become your compass for your everyday life.

> When I feel as if I'm living under a dark cloud,
> I will envision myself walking into the sunshine.

Once you master the art of meditation, you are ready to enjoy the sunshine of fresh perspectives. When you begin acting upon the insights that arise during reflection, an exciting new world of manifesting your special destiny will open to you. Your creative juices will flow, and you will begin incorporating your inner urgings into your daily actions.

You may wish to record some of these insights in your journal. Be sure to date the entries and review them regularly. As you look back at these entries and see how they have changed your spirit and your direction, you will be encouraged that you are embracing your own power to move free.

Make the most of your opening spirit by embracing those people and activities that resonate with you. Pursue that opening that might lead to the educational or professional opportunity you have been seeking. Follow up with that person who inspired you or offered their assistance. Ask for help and advice from others. Doors will begin to open. Cross only those thresholds that feel right to you. Your powerful thoughts will contribute to that new reality. When you feel more hopeful and positive, others will recognize your lightness and be more drawn to you. Over time, your personal and work relationships will transform.

Your newly acquired meditation skills will enable you to spiral up toward your desired life rather than spiraling down into feelings of hopelessness. The joy of new possibilities will wash over you. As you bask in that warmth, your daily life will become more enjoyable. Now you're beginning to move free, generating your own sunshine.

Trail Marker Six: Imagine Moving Free!

Now back to your own joyful journey. The early going might have seemed pretty tough, producing some frustration and impatience in your life and relationships. Your people, both family and friends, may think you have gone off the deep end of late. Some might have preferred that you remain within the familiar old box in which they—and you—felt more comfortable.

Others have chosen to love and accept the authentic you by now, because they recognize a new zest reflected in your eyes. They sense your presence and enjoyment of life. You seem more light-hearted and prone to laughter than before. You are even able to admit and laugh at your foibles. Since I have chosen to become more free-spirited, others are sometimes amazed by my energy and enthusiasm.

When our daughter moved to Chicago for her first post-college job, I rented a truck to move her things. Once the truck was loaded up, I drove it to St. Louis to pick up her roommate and her mother, Marie. We got acquainted over a lovely dinner at their home. Very early the next morning, we met the movers to add her daughter's things to the truck. Marie rode the rest of the way with me. She was impressed that I rented this truck, made all the arrangements for the movers, drove it from Kansas City to Chicago, and acted like the whole thing was a lark. She said to me, "I want what you have." This was during my early post-cancer years, when I was reigniting my adventurous spirit. Apparently, my enthusiasm for what might have seemed a daunting trip was contagious.

Creating Your Own Trail Guide

If you have been following the trail markers, repeating the affirmations to yourself, incorporating them into your life, and journaling your progress, your life undoubtedly feels more effortless and mindful already. Your self-life-coaching journey is getting pretty interesting now. Although you've no doubt integrated some concepts with natural ease and struggled with others, you are beginning to define your own trail guide to moving free. You find it easier to deal with difficulties. You have a more optimistic outlook and are more adventurous than before.

As you continue spending time in reflection and meditation, your intuition is growing. You are developing your personal style of manifesting the life of your dreams. With your new life skills and enthusiasm, you are equipped to imagine and create your own delightful do-over!

Positive manifesting is focusing on what you want in your life and making time to envision those end results. You no longer try to control how and when those outcomes will surface. Instead, you let the details of your life dreams unfold naturally. Your still voice within, guided by your angels, the Holy Spirit, or whatever you call your internal guidance system, is illuminating your path with clarity, direction, and joy—the likes of which you haven't imagined before. A crystal-clear knowing is materializing within your spirit. You are beginning to recognize on a deeper level the best next step for you, in each and every aspect of your new path.

You have come so very far. You have progressed on your ascending hike and can recognize your progress in a number of aspects of your life, including:

- releasing the roadblocks that deterred you
- improving your relationships
- escalating your progress toward your life purpose
- honing your meditation skills
- envisioning your dream life on a regular basis

Cocoons to Wings

Even all those years ago, before we flew,
we shared a feeling, we somehow knew
that our baby spirits would someday take flight.
A metamorphosis began, fanning our inner light.

Our children played, we shared concerns.
We had so very much to learn
about being who we truly were,
about living life on our own terms.

We were far too busy with the busy-ness of life,
consumed with responsibility and strife.
But our cocoons were translucent,
we glimpsed the light—the promise of a future flight.

We were restless to escape the dark,
more anxious still to unfurl our wings.
We chipped away at those entrapping shells,
as best we could during those early years.

The day finally came when the time was right:
we escaped our cocoons and took to flight.
Now we're *moving free and flying high*—
a more expansive view of earth in sight.

Our empty sheaths lie earthbound and still.
We've spread our wings—gravity's lost its appeal
As we flutter on high, we've come to share
the freedom of living with far less care.

For butterflies we were meant to be
and butterflies
are we!

The original version of this poem was inspired by the journeys my friend Paula and I shared. Of course, we certainly didn't take flight overnight. There was a great deal of tedious crawling while we learned to move free. We supported each other as we juggled our demanding roles as wives, mothers, and career women. We enjoyed our share of laughter and tears along the way as we walked alongside each other, especially during some of the more daunting detours on our parallel paths.

While on a recent nature walk, I stopped to observe a caterpillar. I am obsessed with butterflies because they move free, but I had never taken time to study the caterpillar, the beginnings of a butterfly. Even though the caterpillar is only a lowly worm, of sorts, I observed that it appeared to be lighter than other worms, flaunting its fluffy fur. Can you imagine a slimy slug morphing into a butterfly? Neither can I. So, it's not a huge leap to imagine why the caterpillar, in particular, seems destined to find its wings.

Discover Your Wings

As thinking humans, we struggle, plan, and schedule ourselves, believing we can *make* our lives happen. Does the caterpillar try to rush its metamorphosis? I think not. He is content to take a leisurely crawl in the sunshine, completely oblivious to the lovely fate that awaits him.

Much wisdom can be divined from observing nature. While making our way to moving free, we cannot speed up the process or predict how our life will unfold. But when we are truly open to life's possibilities, they will manifest in surprising ways, exceeding our wildest imaginings.

Remember that if you follow your intuition and choose to be expansive in your thoughts and actions, it is only a matter of time until you discover your own wings. You are distinct and special. You have amazing gifts to share with the world. You too have the capacity to fly—to move free. What will you choose?

As you discover your wings, you will view the world from loftier heights. Expect some mountaintop moments as you incorporate these final mantras into your life journey.

> Day by day I'll *go with the flow,*
> allowing my journey to unfold as intended.

You are beginning to incorporate the magical mysteries of moving free into your life. Your personal metamorphosis has begun. As you greet each day with both acceptance and anticipation, you are truly going with the flow of your experience here on earth.

You have given up on your set-in-stone plans, which never fulfilled your rigid expectations anyway. Now you are focusing on what you desire, but stopping short of trying to dictate the details of how and when your dreams will come to fruition. What a relief!

Now that you are moving free, you are equipped to handle challenging circumstances with more patience, confidence, and ease. You will navigate through your detours and recapture your natural joy and peace by meditating and repeating your mantras.

You are vigilantly watching for signs and following the fork in the road that feels right to you. You are acting upon serendipitous opportunities. You are often pleasantly surprised when the answers to perplexing situations suddenly dawn on you. Doors open, and your life flows more effortlessly when you trust your instincts. You are more confident in your core awareness. You have begun to insist on pursuing your own life, hopes, and dreams. In order to move free every day, you must hold fast to this deeper sense of yourself.

> To each his own. To each his own.
> *To each his own!*

Knowing what you believe and why is crucial to discovering your sense of empowerment and direction. Speaking your truth and setting boundaries around your beliefs is freeing. Your spiritual beliefs, politics, and choices in relationships and life work are unique to you and are ever evolving. No one can steal your innate right to determine your personal life path. You must insist that others accept "your own" in all aspects of your life.

Even when you are living in close proximity with others, your heart, soul, thoughts, hopes, and dreams are still yours—all yours. My father tried to dictate my every action during my childhood. I escaped his heavy hand enough to cling to my free spirit within. Even if your physical movement is restricted in certain circumstances, like being incarcerated or disabled, you may still choose to move free within your spirit.

The flip side is that when dealing with others, you must return the favor by accepting them as they are. We each have the right to live as we wish and be true to our beliefs. We must also allow others to embrace that right for themselves.

Remember that this straightforward tenet is the key to emancipating yourself and others, as you each discover your own true trek. How liberating both for you and for those fortunate people with whom you share your free-flowing life.

> We all are one. We all are one.
> *We all are one!*

Although this affirmation may sound contradictory to the previous one, it certainly isn't. We each must be true to who we are. But we truly are the "family of man." Reaching out to all people of the world manifests joy, love, and unity.

Acceptance of all of humankind creates trust and a willingness to co-exist—for the greater good. We must understand that others' beliefs may be vastly different from ours, according to the circumstances in which they grew up and now live. The fact is, we are all in this together, especially when it comes to saving our earth and the world economy from disaster. The ravages of war devastate countries and destroy economies. I believe that we must empathize with our brothers' and sisters' struggles and do our best to be part of the global solution rather than the problem. Discrimination based on race, religion, nationality, socio-economics, sexual preference, or other differences only creates more hatred in the world.

I have learned to expect the best from others and interact with them in a manner of acceptance whenever possible. I have found that if you greet someone with a smile and a pleasant hello, they may respond in a similar fashion. Even if they look shocked or even scowl in response, I am not discouraged. As I venture into the world, I attempt to treat others as equals, because I believe they are. When I demonstrate non-judgment, mutual understanding becomes possible.

This inclusiveness and its effect is demonstrated in the way our servicemen and women reach out to the women and children in countries with whom we are at war—to create a sense of oneness whenever possible. In some circumstances, they are able to play

Moving Free

with the children and help build schools and generally demonstrate that we aren't the "Ugly Americans" that some of their countrymen depict. My constant prayer is that the children currently populating the earth will create a more peaceful world vision for the future.

The religious wars in Ireland demonstrate such a transformation. The previous generations fought and killed each other over religious differences between Catholics and Protestants. I believe this generation of young people finally saw the folly in that ill-placed hatred and refused to fight over it any longer. They haven't eliminated all prejudice and segregation—but at least they aren't shedding blood over it. It's an encouraging first step.

No matter where we come from or what our personal beliefs are, as humans we all face similar struggles and joys. We all enjoy laughter and a child's moments of glee. We all yearn to love and be loved. We all grieve the loss of a loved one. We all experience celebrations and devastations in our lives. We all seek to have peaceful homes. We all would welcome world peace.

When monumental disasters occur, humans band together to save people and the built and natural environments. I believe calamities occur to force people to collaborate with others in order to weather environmental and economic devastation. I believe we can and will become more accepting of others as our eyes open to the necessity for worldwide unity. We will eventually embody the idea that we all are one!

> *Moving free* is, quite simply, reawakening
> my natural free spirit within.

We all came into this world with a free spirit, a natural curiosity, and a zest for life. Everything was a discovery. As youngsters, we marveled at everyone and everything in our life. But soon enough, we learned to curtail our enthusiasm and conform to others' standards. Conformity has its place in our society, workplace, and schools, but we sometimes become so enmeshed in our usual way of doing things that our natural inclination to enjoy our surroundings is stifled.

Wouldn't it be great if we could reawaken our free spirit and our sense of awe? The thing is, we can. We can practice moving free by being still and visualizing ourselves doing what we love. When we respond to signs and open doors with positive action, we are converting what we may have once considered to be a dream life into a life within reach.

Recapturing our free spirit within requires us to embrace some do-over decisions and actions into our lives, including:

- Releasing our woulda, coulda, shouldas
- Resisting others' attempts to control us
- Rejecting others' desire for drama
- Recharging our enthusiasm for our career
- Reenergizing our natural sense of excitement
- Rejoicing in the respite this present moment offers
- Reawakening our child-like joy

> Whenever possible, I intend to *re-zest myself!*

You are gathering momentum and recapturing your child-like enthusiasm. Remind yourself that if you can visualize it, you can create your own shiny new outlook—one in which laughter and playfulness abound.

It's Time to Play!

The joy of the dolphins as they leap and play—
why can't we learn to frolic that way?
For playing doesn't cost a dime
all that's required is to make some time.

When we work, we work
to pay our way.
But when our work is done
it's time to play!

Glimpsing dolphins gliding in the sea
opens your hearts to a bit more glee.
But if you're landlocked, that's okay.
You can always find a way.

Playing fetch with a dog will do the trick.
Or teasing a cat with a feather on a stick.
Take a child to the park and watch him play.
Each spirit lifts us up in its own way!

So ask yourself this serious query.
Do I toil so much it makes me weary?
Or do I make some time to laugh and play
every new surprising day?

It is your choice whether to grasp spontaneous moments of fun or to let them slip away. If you over-schedule your leisure time, you may miss such opportunities. Especially during times of adversity, don't deny yourself a brief respite to renew your spirit. Once a difficult situation has passed, treat yourself to a carefree activity or interaction. Embracing your light-heartedness provides balance in your life and relationships.

Since the birth of our grandson Ethan, spending time with him is the greatest joy imaginable. The first words I taught him were, "Oh, wow!" He still declares his pleasure in new activities and sights with this phrase. I recently fulfilled one of my bucket list desires when he and his parents joined us on the Gulf of Mexico. I watched him take his first steps in the sand and dip his toes in the ocean. He was also captivated by a musician at a dinner venue and even danced with me for the first time. These were magical moments. My spirit soared with delight!

> When I open the eyes of my heart, I might just see something that will *dazzle me.*

Be vigilant for moments of wonder that arise. Discover something that gets your joyful juices flowing. Dabble in new activities that intrigue you. (Hint: You won't find dazzling experiences while curling up on your sofa.) And it isn't necessarily expensive to create captivating moments. Take a chance. Step outside your box. Venture forth. Volunteer to help others. Greet a stranger who intrigues you. Try a different sport or hobby. Sharing such dazzling moments with your friends and loved ones is a wonderful way of connecting with them.

A moment of wonder surprised me when I was visiting Paula in Belize. I knew there were dolphins in those waters, but had not yet encountered one. Every morning at sunrise I would scurry to a pier close to her house. I would do my yoga practice and envision a dolphin appearing. It seemed that my visions wouldn't be fulfilled. On the last morning, I was amazed when a single dolphin appeared on the horizon and swam directly toward me. He came within fifteen yards of me and swam in a u-shaped pattern around both sides of the dock. When he returned to the center of the pier, he paused, rose in the water, and looked directly into my eyes. Then he simply turned and glided away into the depths of the sea. I could scarcely believe it. He responded to my silent call and blessed me with his greeting. I was giddy for days. This experience isn't that surprising, however, when you realize that we are all connected—all people, animals, plants, the earth, the sky, and the entire universe.

> Precious day by precious day, I intend to *appreciate my life* in a conscious way!

Appreciating every day is vital to moving free. When things go our way or opportunities appear, we must celebrate those situations. Say a quick prayer of gratitude when a lovely day or interaction presents itself. Hug and thank a friend for a relaxing outing or exchange. Being consciously grateful for moments of joy manifests more of the same in our lives. What a simple and uplifting concept.

Living in a climate that fluctuates from very cold to very hot, I adore the spring and summer months. I am so grateful for a warm, sunny day that I try to spend as much time outside as possible. I relish eating dinner with Craig or reading a book on our balcony. I enjoy the sunshine as I edit my writing on the patio of a coffee shop. Or sometimes I walk in a favorite park alone or with friends. Nature provides a soothing balm for my spirit.

> I aspire to achieve balance within my mind, body, and spirit, realizing that each part of me yearns to *move free*.

I have devoted most of this book to moving free within our minds and spirits. But moving free in our bodies is also of utmost importance. In order to liberate ourselves completely, we must address our physical as well as our emotional and spiritual aspects.

Practicing yoga, walking, having massages, and dancing with abandon have all been liberating activities for me. I gradually learned to appreciate, nourish, heal, and cherish this vessel that allows me to move freely in the physical world. Losing an extra thirty pounds that was dragging me down was a lovely bonus.

I couldn't have reached the summit of my own true trek without first improving my health, strength, and flexibility. I relied on skilled teachers to help me synchronize my physical and spiritual aspects. Being grounded in my body—being more physically present—was crucial to my spiritual growth. The expression "head in the clouds" described me to a T. In my yoga practice I learned to center myself by following my breath and meditating. And trust me, this was no easy task. Improving my fitness, nutrition, and wellness has dramatically changed my energy and outlook.

Experiment with different types of movement until you recognize what feels good to you. Whatever type of exercise you choose, move your body daily. Feel your muscles toning, stress melting, and endorphins surging.

We must each find our own nutritional formula, but I have learned that the basics of better health through nutrition are fairly straightforward. My advice is this: Ditch the junk food and processed foods and consume more nutritious foods such as whole grains, clean protein, nuts, fruits, and veggies. Most importantly, drink plenty of pure water. Gradually reduce your intake of caffeine, sodas (especially diet versions), and alcoholic beverages as your taste for water grows. Find a cleanse system that works for you and detox regularly. Embrace those nutritional modalities that suit your lifestyle. What a great gift to yourself.

> Saying yes to myself reveals the most direct path to *moving free* in my mind, body, and spirit!

We learned about the importance of asking ourselves how we wish to spend our time in Trail Marker Three. That question is equally important in determining your leisure activities. Achieving a more expansive personal life requires continual reevaluation.

Saying yes to yourself reveals the most direct path toward moving free. Stop spending so much time fulfilling others' needs. Renew your own soul in whatever practices and hobbies allow you to feel free. Prioritize your time and energy. Do your chores efficiently, so you have time to reward yourself. Take a break when you feel the need. Give yourself a spirit lift when you feel bogged down or sad.

Learn to sometimes say no to others so you can say yes to your own desires. Yes to your sense of peace. Yes to time and space for stillness. Yes to your creative urges. Yes to talking with someone who lifts you up. Yes to music that soothes your spirit. Yes to spending time in nature and feeling the warmth of the sun on your face.

As you reinforce your right to say no, your schedule will ease, leaving more moments to celebrate each day. Indulge in the pleasure of free time to renew yourself. Accept only those invitations that appeal to you. Choose people, books, movies, and television programs that lift you up rather than feed your anxiety. Spend time with friends and loved ones who share your enthusiasm for life. Deeply reconnect with your significant other.

Spur-of-the-moment, uplifting activities will spark your joy. When you feel tethered, engage in an activity or spend time in a place that refreshes your spirit. Remind yourself that doing so isn't selfish. It's simply nurturing yourself so your light will shine forth.

The more time you spend doing what you value and releasing activities and situations that run counter to your sense of joy, the more you embrace your personal freedom. The headiness of liberating yourself physically, emotionally, and spiritually surfaces as you consciously choose how to spend your time. It's never too late to pursue interests that intrigue you: playing an instrument, singing, dancing, sports, artistic expression, photography, or other activities.

I didn't become the master of my own destiny until my empty nest years. When I retired from my sales career, I had time to reevaluate my personal activities and relationships. I relinquished those that no longer resonated with me in order to free my time and energy for social situations that fit my new life vision. I gave up overly structured clubs when they began to feel restrictive. I enjoyed personal connections in deeper ways and pursued new interests and people who fed my spirit. I began to feel lighter as I opted to spend more time relaxing in nature and less time shopping. I chose walking, practicing yoga, and riding my bike over cleaning the house. My enjoyment of my life and relationships blossomed as a result of redirecting my time and energy.

My favorite ways of saying yes to myself are gardening and taking solitary trips to concentrate on my writing. Digging in the dirt and pruning my flowers and vegetables takes my mind off my concerns. Cooking with the herbs and vegetables I grow nourishes both my body and spirit. When I crave alone time to regroup and find my writing voice, I escape to a nearby retreat or to my favorite seaside spots. Nature inspires and calms me. Such interludes allow me the freedom to work day or night uninterrupted and to respond immediately to insights that surface. My thoughts and words flow more freely when I'm not distracted by my regular daily demands.

The Beach—My Muse

Ah—the sacred serenity of the beach at sunrise—
a glorious awakening to another sparkling day.
The expansiveness of the sea engulfs me.
The pelicans gliding and swooping enchant me.

Squishing my toes in the sand is grounding.
The crashing of the waves mesmerizes me,
lulling my breath to echo its ebb and flow.

Daylight grows now, painting the shallow
surf in crimson and pink.
The sea breeze and sunshine warm my
soul, spark fresh thoughts.
Fully awake now—my words flood in—it's time to write.

> I intend to be in sync
> with my own synchronicity

We sync our smart phones with our laptops. We sync our calendars to our smart phones. We spend hours buried in Facebook or various apps. We search out everything and everyone imaginable via the Internet. We go to great lengths in order to remain in sync with the outside world. These tools are invaluable for connecting with faraway friends and family members or researching topics of interest. But this kind of communication is indirect; it lacks the soul-to-soul connection that can be achieved when one is in the presence of another. Spending excessive time on your cell phone, tablet, or laptop may deter you from connecting with your friends and family in a deep way.

While we're on the subject—when you are with other people, meaningful conversation is impossible if you are constantly texting or checking your social media apps. One night my husband and I were eating dinner at a restaurant. Four attractive young women were sitting at a nearby table, dressed to the nines. They were each engrossed in texting other people. There was no conversation going on among them. Instead of connecting with each other, each woman was involved in another conversation with someone who was not at the table, perhaps figuring out where and with whom she would be meeting up next. In other words, they weren't present with each other in a significant way. They might as well have been home alone.

Another concerning effect of technology is that it can become a time waster or even an obsession. When we allow the distraction of cell phones, tablets, and computers to claim our attention, we lose the crucial alone time we need to move free. We lose the opportunity to tune in to our inner space during quiet moments of reflection. The revelation of creative thoughts, positive options, solutions to nagging issues, and bright new perspectives occurs only during times of solitude.

ೞೞೞ

As we become more in sync with our inner urgings, our daily reflections will illuminate our path more brightly. The once subtle shifts in our lives will become more apparent. Our aha-moments will come more frequently and reveal different perspectives. Synergistic opportunities in life will arise to point us in the direction of our dreams. Our proficiency in the art of serendipity will increase as we recognize there are no accidents. Our intuition will reveal surprising new vistas when we trust and act upon them. Our lives will synergistically unfold in magical ways.

A concrete knowing of the right next step? Yes, it's coming into view now. The courage and resilience to step out in a new direction? It's building. Unexpected opportunities? They are beginning to feel as natural as can be. Talk about an ascending journey!

As I honed my meditating skills, I began to recognize and act upon the clear signs my small voice within delivered. I wasn't surprised, but I was thrilled when the perfect person or solution appeared. And where am I now as a result of listening to my inner guidance? My dream of sharing my path to encourage others is coming to fruition.

Meeting *the one* and falling in love is a wonderful example of serendipity. Was meeting Craig by the pool in my apartment complex an accident? I no longer think so. It truly was love at first sight. He felt and looked familiar and comfortable to me. Perhaps we had known each other in another place and time.

Having our children sooner than we had planned was yet another joyous accident. Looking back, I believe they arrived at just the right time. These exciting and sudden turns of events were joyful synergistic opportunities that presented themselves early in my adult years. I am glad I responded with openness and excitement. Once I recovered from the shock, that is.

My author coach Diane started her consulting business while continuing to work for a large publisher. Not long after she began editing my book and learning about moving free, she resigned from that firm. Her boss encouraged her to stay, promising he would make it worth her while. She suddenly blurted out, "No—I have to move on!" Her strong declaration surprised her, but then she laughed at herself. Several weeks later she phoned to tell me she was literally experiencing the joy of moving free!

Sometimes we learn what we don't want in our own lives by observing others' tragic outcomes. Such was the case following my mother's passing. I knew I didn't want to wait until my final day to move free. Recognizing and acting upon this revelation didn't happen overnight. It has taken years for me to fully embrace her accidental legacy, but it sparked my journey toward moving free in my mind, body, and spirit.

When a sudden tragic accident or devastating illness comes out of the blue, we may eventually realize that our earlier lifestyle or choices set us on a path toward calamity long before it manifested. Making wiser decisions in the future will create more desirable outcomes. When we align our actions with our instincts, we are able to move in the direction of our dreams.

The bottom line is that both the most joyful and the most devastating circumstances in our lives serve to illuminate our pathway. But we must grasp the lessons of such situations in order to grow.

> I choose to *be expansive* in my thoughts and actions!

In order to incorporate new perspectives and directions, we must listen to our inner voice. Most importantly, we need to be flexible enough to embrace the changes needed to follow that illuminated path we've glimpsed. We need to expand our thoughts to consider new possibilities.

Now that we have the skills to retreat to our inner space, we can reset our intention and reclaim our tranquility and joy. We can choose to replace old thought patterns with more expansive ones. By going within. By finding a place of ease. By breathing out our fear of the unknown and breathing in our serenity.

We are becoming more capable of releasing rigidity in our life choices and relationships. We are choosing to be more elastic, like a rubber band. As we do so, our connections will flow more effortlessly, abounding in laughter, love, and joy.

The circumstances of our lives seldom unfold as we expect. The twists and turns of our paths are numerous. But each reveals surprising perspectives and opportunities for growth, if we are flexible enough to notice and respond to them. We are free to embrace a do-over, today and every day, gliding on the wings of our personal freedom.

> Today, I intend to float downstream,
> *going with the flow* of the smoother waters
> I've manifested into my life.

Just when we think things are flowing smoothly, life can present some daunting rapids. They may appear quite suddenly, catching us off-guard as we round a bend. Some of these surprises are unavoidable. There is no turning back. We must lean into the current and courageously navigate through it. Remember that we may discover some gems of wisdom or develop new skills of navigation as a result of our rough ride.

Once we arrive in more tranquil waters, we will relish the chance to pull in the oars and comfortably float for a while, fully appreciating the smoother ride. We will find ourselves carried on the current of our hopes and desires. Floating downstream is ever so much sweeter. Going with the flow of our lives and trusting when serendipity appears will guide us to the destination of our dreams.

I experienced a life-changing post-cancer enthusiasm. Facing my own mortality and coming out the other side opened my eyes. Suddenly, I was embracing my life with a gratitude and passion that had been missing before my diagnosis. I began appreciating and deepening my connections with my friends and family members. My life and work became more effortless as I reprioritized my relationships. I felt I was truly floating downstream for the first time in my life. I was experiencing the magic of moving free!

> I intend to *move free*
> *right here, right now!*

Moving Free

I will choose expansiveness over rigidity. I will laugh and cry with those I love. I will seek solace and inspiration in nature. I will walk courageously forward, focusing on the God-light ahead. I will pay attention to my signs and intuitive thoughts. I will move free each and every day. I will celebrate my forward momentum. I will share my joyful countenance with others and encourage them to move free in their own way. I intend to add my special spark to the moving free movement that is destined to change our Universe for the better.

ෲෲෲ

- *As you ponder your current life, are you allowing yourself to glimpse the light by trusting your instincts and effortlessly moving toward your destiny? Can you imagine what surprises await if you stop struggling to create your own wings and simply remain vigilant for the openings Spirit has for you? Answer these questions honestly, recording some desired outcomes you wish to manifest into your life.*
- *Looking back, reflect on a situation of loss or a devastating moment—perhaps the loss of a relationship or friendship, the death of a loved one, or a job you left under unpleasant circumstances. In retrospect, what did you learn from that situation? What was the silver lining?*
- *Now think of a current challenging situation. Are you beginning to discover your wings by more readily absorbing lessons and shifting your attention to a more positive outcome?*
- *Next, reflect on some positive instances of synchronicity in your past. Perhaps it was the birth of a child or the discovery of a new friend. Perhaps it was falling in love or finding a new job. What did you learn from those situations? How did you manifest those joys into existence? How can you use those joys to bring more positive light into your life? Record and celebrate some positive synchronicities you have experienced.*

- *Examine what sets you free. Describe in detail your personal vision of moving free. How does it feel? What uplifting emotions are you experiencing? Where are you? Who surrounds you? What are you doing for work and play? What joy and gifts are you sharing with the world as a result?*
- *Review your vision for moving free often and manifest it in your daily intentions and actions!*

PART III

NOW CAN YOU IMAGINE MOVING FREE?

Now Can You Imagine Moving Free?

It has been a long and arduous hike. Your endorphins are finally kicking in and are propelling you forward. Your exhaustion recedes as you realize the final summit is only steps away. The reward for your daunting upward trek is within reach. What in the world is it that you glimpse just ahead? Is it a mirage? No—the shiny white glider plane in front of you is real! You rush toward it and sweep your hands across its sleek, cool surface, realizing this is not a figment of your imagination. What are you waiting for?

Your choice is crystal clear. You have lightened your backpack along the way by removing many of your past fears and doubts. Now you're ready to let go of any remaining baggage that might overload the glider. You remove your backpack from your weary shoulders and drop it right where you stand. What a relief. You allow yourself the deepest sigh you have ever uttered—ahhhh.

You are ready to take a leap of faith. Your time to shine has come. Your very own shimmering glider awaits. It has room for only one passenger—you. As if by magic, you realize that you know exactly how to pilot this graceful craft. Perhaps you have always known how, though you don't recall taking lessons or getting your certification. You hop on board without so much as a backward glance and fasten your seat belt. You don the protective goggles, the helmet, and the crimson silk scarf lying on the seat.

It's your time to gently and effortlessly float on air. Although you know you can't dictate your exact flight plan—it *is* a glider, after all—you feel confident it will be the most glorious ride of your life. You take off without the slightest hesitation. The feeling of weightlessness is exhilarating. The view from this lofty altitude is awe-inspiring. What was once just a dream has come to fruition. You are truly moving free now!

The Ride of Your Life

The glider ride symbolizes the effortlessness you will experience more and more as you incorporate the magical mysteries of moving free into your life. Certainly you will experience bumps in the road, but now that you have released the roadblocks and embraced your renewed enthusiasm and manifesting skills, difficulties won't throw you as far off course as they once did. And the clear guidance you glean from your personal challenges will thrill you.

As you recall from your hiking experiences, the more vertical the uphill climb, the tougher it was to keep going. You may have been forced to stop and catch your breath. The same applies to your emotional and spiritual growth. The steeper path at the beginning of your ascending journey—when you were struggling to understand and integrate the principles of the first few trail markers—was quite challenging.

Once you improved your interactions with others and meditated more often, however, you were able to reach higher peaks of joy with confidence. Moving forward, you'll experience more downhill hikes and fewer uphill battles. Now that you have honed those life skills that enable you to navigate your own twists and turns—both happy and rough—your life journey will exceed your earlier expectations. Your dream work, friends, and life will feel more accessible. Your descents will become surprising joyrides. You will feel giddy as you glide in a spiraling pattern and gently land at the bulls-eye of your bliss.

It's Only a Matter of Time!

Envision your wishes and do your work every day.

When the time is right—you'll find your way

to desired manifestations so very sweet.

When least expected, you will greet

the life of your dreams—

effortlessly

it seems!

Dearest One,

I have been honored to share my sacred journey with you, in order to ease your way. I hope you have found some measure of encouragement and light and that you have gleaned fresh insights from embracing your personal journey with more confidence and zeal. I envision you now anticipating and savoring each surprising day of your life with excitement. For each moment and hour, despite its ups and downs, is indeed precious.

My heartfelt wishes for you are simply these: that you are moving free in your own way—in the direction of your dream life, trusting in your own true trek. That your glider is approaching your intended destination. That your exhilaration is exploding as you clear the clouds. That you are boldly embracing each magical moment, hour, and day of your journey with gratitude and courage. That you are effortlessly floating toward each gentle landing, just as you envisioned you would, in the center of your own life labyrinth.

Now, let your inner light shine. Spread your joy and love to those with whom your share your path. You will surely surprise yourself each magical day as you rise and swoop. In the process, you will dazzle your fellow travelers, adding your unique spark to the growing fire of awakening that is glowing ever more brightly, day by day. That's it! You are moving free, right here, right now!

Light and love,

Deb

Suggested Reading List

Relationships

A Walk on the Beach, Joan Anderson
Codependent No More, Melody Beattie
Eat Pray Love, Elizabeth Gilbert
The Four Agreements, Don Miguel Luis

Awakening and Manifesting

The Isaiah Effect, Gregg Braden
Infinite Possibilities, Mike Dooley
The Top Ten Things Dead People Want to Tell You, Mike Dooley
The Power of Intention Perpetual Flip Calendar, Dr. Wayne W. Dyer
A New Earth, Eckart Tolle
Stillness Speaks, Eckart Tolle
The Power of Now, Eckart Tolle

About the Author

Deb Vaughan Ritter earned her Bachelor's degree in Psychology and juggled her busy life as a successful career woman, wife, and mother for many years. Her mother's final declaration that she "must move free" changed Deb's trajectory. This surprising revelation sparked Deb's desire to discover her own "true trek." Many years of voracious reading, writing, seeking, being in nature, yoga, and meditation followed. Her words naturally flowed as she revealed the secrets of moving free that she gleaned on her transformative journey.

Deb currently moves free in the Kansas City area with her husband, Craig.

Printed in the United States
By Bookmasters